Teaching Infants

Trevor Kerry
Janice Tollitt

Basil Blackwell

© Dr Trevor Kerry and Janice Tollitt 1987
First published 1987

Reprinted 1988

Published by Basil Blackwell Ltd
108 Cowley Road
Oxford OX4 1JF
England

British Library Cataloguing in Publication Data

Kerry, Trevor
 Teaching Infants.
 1. Elementary school teaching 2. Education
 Primary
 I. Title   II. Tollitt, Janice
 372.11'02   LB1511

 ISBN 0-631-15073-0

Typeset by Multiplex techniques ltd
in 10 on 12pt Sabon and 10 on 12pt Gill Sans
Printed in Great Britain
by T. J. Press (Padstow) Ltd

Contents

Index of Tasks

Index of Tables

Acknowledgements

The authors wish to thank Sheila Reilly for giving up part of her summer vacation to type the manuscript. Without her assistance this book would not have met its deadlines. We recognise our debt also to the many heads, teachers and pupils who have shaped our thinking. Any short-comings in the book remain our own.

The authors and publisher would like to thank the following for permission to reproduce copyright material:
Professor Wynne Harlen and Taylor and Francis Ltd. for the diagram on p.109; Mr D. Connor of Etwall Primary School, Derbyshire for the extract from the topic handbook on pp.123–4; Mr. P. Grills of Asterdale Primary School, Derbyshire for the extract from the staff handbook on pp. 125–6; Croom Helm Ltd. for the planning web on p.143 from a chapter by Chris Burke in 'Finding and Helping the Able Child', ed. Trevor Kerry (1983); School Curriculum Development Committee Publications for the extracts by Janice Tollitt on p.148 *et seq.* from 'Topic Work Resource Bank' (1985).

INTRODUCTION

This is a book about teaching infants. It is aimed at teachers of infants and at students in training. We hope it is a distinctive book. Our view is that it is distinctive in three ways.

First, this is a task book. It invites the reader to increase her awareness of professional skills, to work on these skills through seventy practical exercises or tasks, and thus to improve her skills in a conscious and systematic way. This kind of reader-involvement, awareness-raising, and professional self-development activity is not wholly new. But it is unusual to find these methods applied to teaching skills at the infant level of education.

The second distinctive feature of this book is that it makes frequent reference to research or to theoretical underpinning when considering and analysing practical teaching skills. There are precedents for this, of course, but rarely at the infant level of education. We have been struck by the paucity of skills-based materials for teachers of infants. Most of the practical literature for teachers of this age-group is couched in the 'tips for teachers' format or is tacked on as an after-thought to volumes about the primary school.

Third, this is a book that tries actively to promulgate a particular view of the infants' teacher. It may be true that the public is becoming more aware that teachers of young children are not failed or less competent teachers of older ones, but if so there has been little progress beyond that. The draft proposal for this volume was rejected by one publisher on the grounds that 'infants' teachers cannot cope with references'. The editor concerned in making this judgement was quite unable to see the irony of the revelation that many potential readers would be graduates or undergraduates of honours BEd courses. But this book has been compiled with that recognition: that teachers of infants should demand recognition as highly trained, intellectually rigorous professionals.

If we have fulfilled our aims in putting together a task-based skills book for teachers of infants, then there are some things the reader should expect to find on the pages that follow and some she should not. We hope that there will be no jargon. We have tried to avoid the trap of compiling sample lessons for direct implantation into your own classroom (most ready-made lessons will be inappropriate!) We have not been prescriptive over teaching method since there is no golden mean of behaviour applicable to all infant classrooms in all circumstances. There is no such thing as a perfect lesson.

Instead, we have attempted to isolate some key skills and issues in infant education. The book is divided into Units, each Unit focusing on a major theme and its related sub-themes. The Units are self-contained for the sake of clarity, but are often inter-related or cross-referenced since teaching skills operate in a context of varying human behaviour, not as isolated and mechanical phenomena. Within each Unit there are tasks for the reader to carry out either in her own classroom, as opportunity arises, or on teaching practice. Often the tasks require the assistance of fellow-professionals. This is because for too long, teaching has been a relatively private and autonomous activity whereas true professional development requires sharing of others' wisdom and the contribution of one's own. The text is confined to fairly short blocks wherever possible, and much information is tabulated. Our hope is that this layout will permit busy teachers to use the book selectively to fulfil their own needs, and to utilise sections of it in an already busy professional programme; for, above all, this book is classroom-based and task-orientated. To read the volume from cover to cover would serve some purpose, but the true value lies in carrying out the tasks and reflecting on them.

We have collected references at the back of the book. In this way they leave the text uncluttered, but are there for those who may wish to follow up specific topics as and when the need arises. It is particularly important for teachers of young children to sharpen their minds on occasion by deliberate study at their own level.

The feminine gender is used in referring to the teacher throughout the book because we recognise that most teachers of young children are as a matter of fact female. The pronoun 'she' is in all other ways value-free and devoid of sexist connotations of any kind!

The psychologist B F Skinner once described education as 'what survives when what has been learned has been forgotten'. This book is offered in that spirit: the wisdom you acquire from completing the tasks should outlast the information printed on these pages. In this way you will have become the agent of your own professional advancement.

Unit 1

WHAT KIND OF TEACHER?

Teaching small children is a very demanding occupation calling for reserves of mental and physical energy as well as considerable creative flair. When we discuss infant education we have to remember that we are concerned with the child's first ever impressions of schools and teachers. Thus, what we are, what we do, and the environment we create may be formative for the pupil's whole future attitude towards education. In the quotations that follow we see this process of attitude formation in progress.

'We marched up a long gravel drive to a red-brick building, with iron railings excluding the world on either side. Boisterous children were playing boisterous games, boys in one playground and girls in another, penned like prisoners in the yards, by bars shut in. A severe woman of great height, half-hidden behind brown glasses that concealed the natural shape of her eyes, peered menacingly down at me. Seizing me by the hand, she released my mother's grip on me and suddenly I was alone with this big person with a big voice...I cried.'

'That school was like an Aladdin's cave of mystery and warm colours. The pastel paint of the corridor, lined with low shelves spilling over with tempting books, led to a hall with a carpeted corner where would-be bookworms could curl up in a cold winter's lunchtime. Round the walls life-size Vikings went on raids, and bunches of crepe-paper flowers decorated its piano top. I never passed that hall without lingering, and Miss Roberts the headmistress would call 'hello' from her office door, or ask me to read a sentence, or point out some new treasure on the nature table, or smile and ask me how my older sister was getting on in the juniors.'

Task I Remembering your earliest experiences of school

1   Write a short and truthful account of your own earliest memories of school –
the first day, and first impressions of your teacher.
2   Ask some colleagues or friends to describe their first days at school and their
earliest memory of the teacher.
3   List some of the key words (positive and negative) they use in their descriptions
of both the school and the teacher, thus:

	Positive words	Negative words
SCHOOL		
TEACHER		

4   What do your findings tell you about pupils' first encounters with schools and
teachers, and about the impressions they leave?
5   What conclusions would you draw about pupils' first encounters with school?

Table 1 lists some characteristics commonly identified by educationists as
desirable in an effective teacher of infants. Study the list and carry out Task 2.

TABLE I Some characteristics of an effective infants' teacher	
Characteristics: a good teacher of infants will...	Example of this during the lesson observed in Task 2
provide a safe psychological climate	
be fair and consistent in dealing with lapses from good behaviour	
know each child individually by name	

show a knowledge of children's background
be aware of individual learning needs
accept children's initiatives in work or activities
get down physically to the children's level
cope with a variety of tasks in progress simultaneously
organise transitions from one activity to another quickly and without fuss
provide a range of exciting sensory experiences in the classroom
encourage warm classroom relationships between pupils
provide a wide range of commercial and teacher-produced resources

Task 2 Watching an infants' teacher at work

1   Find the opportunity to watch an infants' teacher at work, preferably one whom you believe to have excellent relations with the children. Use Table 1 to focus your observations of her behaviour. Record in the right-hand column of the

Table one or more examples of each of the characteristics listed there which occurs during the lesson.
2   Are there any characteristics you would add to the list in the left-hand column? What are they?
3   What insights have you gained from this Task?

One recurrent educational debate which has tended to centre on the primary school concerns the question: which are more effective, formal or informal teaching methods? The debate was highlighted in recent years by Neville Bennett's *Teaching styles and pupil progress* (Open Books, 1976). Bennett's thesis suggested more effective learning *tended* to take place in formal classrooms; but his statistical methods have been called into question regularly, and current opinion suggests the case is unproven on the evidence. Nevertheless, the question of teaching style is a significant one.

According to Bennett, children taught by formal teachers tended to make more progress in reading and numeracy. But there are, as he concedes, complicating factors. Thus, in a school where reading occupies 50 minutes each day pupils will, in general, make more reading progress than in one where it occupies 30 minutes daily. Whether this reading activity comes about in 'reading lessons' or through meeting spontaneous needs may be less important in determining the learning gain than is the time factor itself. What is important is the relative value placed on reading by the teacher in school.

In this book we shall not pursue directly the debate about formal versus informal teaching. Rather, we shall advocate a balanced approach, drawing on what is best in both methods to provide an effective blend of teaching approaches which is flexible enough to be evolved by the user into her own personal style. Similarly we shall attempt to promote awareness of effective methods of teaching in various domains (affective, aesthetic, cognitive) while leaving room for manoeuvre in the teacher's personal development of a value system for infant education.

Unit 2

CLASSROOM ORGANISATION

We have seen already that an effective teacher of infants will be someone whose work and surroundings will be well organised, exciting and stimulating, and will contain the resources and materials necessary to sustain learning. In Task 2 you watched a teacher exploiting some of these skills and facilities. The precise way in which you organise your own surroundings for learning will depend upon their nature (eg whether the school is open plan or has traditional box classrooms) and scope (the shape and dimensions, and such factors as accessibility to electric points). Here we shall try to examine some principles which the teacher can apply to her own circumstances, first with respect to the classroom or teaching area. Carry out Task 3.

Task 3 Exploring space

1   Draw out a plan (scale approx 3 cm—1 metre) of your own facilities: classroom/ teaching space, store areas, cloakrooms etc. Include fixed items and heavy furniture which can't be moved.
2   Take stock of what is available, eg
>   floor area
>   wall-space
>   notice boards
>   black- or whiteboard
>   storage space
>   horizontal surfaces
>   ceiling beams

bays
windows and the views from them
'wet' areas (sinks etc)
adjacent corridors
location of electric points
other facilities (add them here)

3   Now consider carefully if you are using each of these facilities effectively. The small sample of exploratory ideas in Table 2 will start you thinking.

TABLE 2 Exploiting space	
Floor area	Layout of tables, chairs etc will have an effect upon kinds of activities you can employ – think of spaces for individual work, group activity, story-time and so on.
Wall space	By using Blu-tac etc, can this be exploited for display – of children's work, of stimulus materials, of resource materials around a topic of current concern?
Noticeboards	Fixing devices can be more varied here (staple guns, pins). Possible use for more long-term items, eg 'word ladders' of basic vocabulary, packs of stimulus cards giving tasks for pupils with 'free' moments.
Black/whiteboards	Up-dated display of day, date, season, clock-face. 'Word a day' reinforcement.
Storage area	Think out problems of access, cleanliness, lay-out. If unsightly, how can area be disguised? eg doorway 'dressed' as time machine, or attractively curtained.
Horizontal surfaces	Useful for equipment (magnifying glass, Lego etc), specimens, 3D artefacts made by children, 3D displays by teacher, plants.
Ceiling beams	In older schools it may be practical to use these as hangers for 'word trees', mobiles, etc.
Bays	Can these be pressed into service as a reading corner, a group-work area, a wet area, a project base?

Windows & views	Art work can often be displayed effectively when back-lit by window light. Window may look out on to field, with potential for watching wildlife, or onto school yard with bird-feeder.
Wet areas	As well as supporting art work, cookery etc these areas give potential for scientific experiments, volume and quantity work, keeping an aquarium etc.
Adjacent corridors	Can be decorated to harmonise with any theme developed in the classroom, eg some may lend themselves to open access bookshelves and browsing areas.
Electric points	Enable a range of audiovisual aids to be used in teaching and learning. Pupils can operate tape-recorders or simple slide viewers, so increasing potential for individual or group work, or helping non-readers.

4   Put into effect some of the ideas evolving from your deliberations.
5   REMEMBER two important principles:
    a.   Once you have reorganised your room, have an eye to the total *visual impact* it creates.
    b.   This whole process (1–4) will need to be repeated at *regular intervals* or your room will grow stale again. Needs change, and your environment should evolve in sympathy to satisfy them.

Space is essentially a learning resource. Managing space is a key skill for an infants' teacher. Much of that management is about

- providing opportunities for a variety of child-centred but teacher-directed activities (story-time);
- reinforcing children's more formal work through real experience or play (eg through display, or in the classroom shop);
- setting up opportunities for tactile or imaginative play as an aid in itself (sand, water, building blocks);
- making available the essential resources that pupils need in order to learn;
- creating an environment conducive to spontaneous learning.

These five principles are illustrated in more detail in the slide sequence associated with this book, details of which are available from Trans-Ed Copying Services, 15 Lady Bower Close, North Hykeham, Lincoln, LN6 8EX. We can also explore them in the following quotation from a teacher talking about her management of classroom space.

> 'In the classroom I have a display board with a series of cards on it. The children spend quite a lot of time in groups according to their age and stage; these groups have animal names – lions, tigers, bears and so on. On the display board, each day, I put up the "group pictures" followed by cards depicting a sequence of tasks. So today, a child in the lions' group will begin with reading, while the tigers are using number apparatus and the bears are at the paint tables. After morning break, the tasks change, and the children know where to go next by consulting the cards; this way I can concentrate on monitoring or on having apparatus ready and the children organise themselves with very little fuss.
>
> 'In the same way, you'll notice that there are a lot of wall displays that the children consult, like this word ladder. On the ladder are the twelve words most commonly in use, according to authorities like Moyle. The children continually focus on these words. In fact, at the beginning of the year we focused on one word a week and the children each had a personal word ladder. They climbed the ladder rung by rung by learning a word at a time.
>
> 'The class shop serves a similar purpose. When an individual child has finished his or her immediate task, rather than face dead time he or she can "go to the shop". There are shopping lists and plastic money near by. The child buys some goods, finds the cost and works out his change. The whole structure of the classroom is designed not to occupy pupils but to set up a constant series of enjoyable but purposeful activities. By thinking ahead I can free myself of many organisational chores to concentrate on checking what and how children are learning.'

The context in which the management of spaces takes place will, of course, vary from school to school. The most important variable is whether or not a school is open plan. It is not usually possible to change a traditional school into an open plan, nor easy effectively to make the opposite transition. But the issue is one which will tax the minds both of students about to go on teaching practice or start a first job, and of teachers seeking a new appointment or promotion. Table 3 looks at the pros and cons of open plan schools.

Traditional schools can be made more 'open' in approach by employing one or more of the following means:

- using team teaching
- having communal areas (eg a library) in use by several groups at once
- making flexible use of year-group structures

TABLE 3 Aspects of the open plan school	
Advantages	*Disadvantages*
1 Staff can be used more flexibly	1 Classes don't have a fixed identity
2 It encourages team-teaching	2 The noise level in the school is too high
3 Space is not divided territorially	3 It wastes a lot of time in movement and organisation
4 It makes better use of scarce equipment and resources	4 Children can more easily cover up when they are not working
5 Individual staff become facilitators	5 Teachers lack the convenience and security of a 'home base'
6 Teachers' specialist skills can reach a wider audience of pupils	6 Maintaining discipline is more difficult
7 There is a more effective use of total floor space for education as opposed to administration or circulation	7 Lesson preparation is more difficult
	8 It is a retrograde step, back to the 'village school' concept
8 It is cheaper to build	
9 It makes pupils more independent	9 Staff are not adequately trained to use effectively the teaching methods demanded by open-plan buildings

The Schools' Council Project 'Open Plan Schools' is discussed in a book of that title by
N Bennett, J Andreae, P Hegarty and B Wade
(NFER Publishing Company, 1980)

- sharing topics or themes across the school
- visiting the junior classes which pupils will eventually enter
- facilitating formal and informal communication between head and staff, and between staff colleagues.

Thus, openness as an attitude of mind is of more significance than the physical lay-out of a building: this again is an important principle of organisation for learning. The Tudor poet Andrew Marvell used the description 'a fine and private place' of the grave; he might just as aptly have used it of certain classrooms in some of today's schools! In each case the privacy has a distinct scent of decay.

Finally in this Unit we return to the affective considerations on which so much effective infant teaching depends to advocate the following principle: that space has to be managed to provide a sound climate in which adult-pupil and pupil-pupil relationships can flourish and where psychological security is high. Ask yourself, for example how you would handle each of the following situations.

Where appropriate, use the scale plan you produced in Task 3 to help you plan.

- It is the first school day for a new intake of children, how are you going to make them (and their parents) feel welcome?
- A talented parent offers to help you one afternoon a week by providing simple Needlework or Craft skills. How will you integrate her into your classroom?
- You discover that you are going to receive a student Nursery Nurse in a week's time. What plans will you make to use her?
- The children have been watching a new television series at home and seem obsessed with monsters. Some are frightened. How can you exploit your room and its facilities to help them to face and overcome these fears?

Unit 3

GROUPING FOR LEARNING

The purpose of this Unit is to examine two questions:

How are pupils assigned to learning groups?

Why are they grouped in these ways?

Before we explore these questions further you might like to think about the grouping practices that occur in your own school and in your classroom by carrying out Task 4.

Task 4 Grouping for learning

1 Take a look at the structure of your own school: the number of pupils on roll, the number of classes into which they are divided, the age and/or ability criteria which inform this division into classes. It might help to draw a diagram of the school organisation showing this information.

2 Now consider your own classroom. Note the age-range of pupils in your class. What mechanisms do you use to assign the children to working groups eg age, sex, ability, interest? Do you use a variety of methods?

3 Take each of the grouping methods you have listed in response to 2 above, and say why you use it and under what circumstances.

Task 4 has helped you to isolate the grouping methods and criteria you use regularly. If you keep your responses to hand as you work through this section you will be able to compare your situation with the practice of other professionals. We shall begin by looking at the organisation of the whole school.

Mixed age classes

A typical village school of the 1880s would have been housed in a large single-roomed barn of a building and have contained one class of pupils, ages ranging from admission to departure. Fashion changed, and pupils became grouped into 'annual' age-bands. But the mixed age class, for reasons we shall explore shortly, reappeared as *vertical grouping*. To explore this phenomenon Bennett (Bennett et al 1982) undertook an investigation into mixed age or vertically grouped classes, the interim findings from which have been used in parts of this Unit.

Vertical groups can be found in all kinds of infant and primary schools. In Bennett's survey (carried out in the NW of England) 54% of infant schools (sample size n = 136), 100% of first schools (n = 5) and 77% of combined junior and infant schools (n = 647) claimed to have at least some mixed age classes. It was thought that a major reason for this form of organisation was falling rolls: as numbers of pupils dropped and staff were cut, few organisational alternatives were left. Indeed, of the infant schools in the sample 50.7% claimed that vertical groups were the outcome of necessity, and in combined junior and infant schools as many as 73.9% made the same claim! In later stages of their work Bennett and his associates limited the definition of mixed age classes so as to include only those with at least two age-levels of pupils, each represented by a third of children in the class. Even so, 26% of infant *schools* were found to have half or more of their classes vertically grouped; and in infant *departments* this figure rose to 50.6%. Though the decision to convert to mixed age classes was usually taken by head and staff in consultation – even parents were involved in the decision-making in some instances – only 37% of staff in infant schools reported themselves committed to this form of organisation, and 40.2% in J&I schools. About 13% of staff in each kind of school reported themselves positively hostile, while the rest felt varying degrees of neutrality.

Task 5 Assessing the effectiveness of vertical grouping

1   If your school operates a vertical grouping system carry out a survey of your involved colleagues asking them the following questions:
  - How was the decision to re-organise in this way made?
  - Why was it made? (List as many reasons as possible).
  - What are your own personal feelings about this form of organisation?
  - What educational advantages does mixed age grouping bring to the children?
  - What educational disadvantages does mixed age grouping impose upon the children?
  - What social advantages or disadvantages does this form of organisation have?
  - What problems does mixed age grouping create for you as a teacher? (eg in preparation, classroom organisation etc.)

2   If you do not have any vertical grouping in your school, imagine that your headteacher has just announced a change to this form of organisation from next September. Make a list of the problems you would anticipate.
3   After carrying out exercise 1 or exercise 2 above, compare your findings or deliberations with the list of possible problems given below in Table 4.

TABLE 4 Some possible problems associated with mixed age school organisation

- Some staff may not be sufficiently experienced or committed to cope with it.

- Parents may be suspicious of its effects on their children's progress.

- It may be a way of increasing class size or of sustaining over-size classes.

- This form of organisation may be thought to be based on political or economic criteria rather than educational ones.

- It may increase the need for the quantity and range of resources available in individual classrooms.

- It may demand more individual attention for pupils than teachers have time to give.

- Less able children may just sink through lack of individual attention.

- Brighter/older pupils may be insufficiently stimulated.

- The school buildings may be unsuitable.

- Staff may not have a sufficient range of teaching methods at their finger-tips to work effectively in this context.

- There may be increased behaviour problems.

- It may cause stress to staff.

- There may be an increased administrative demand on staff eg to keep records of pupil progress.

- The pupils may not like it.

As a postscript to this section on mixed age grouping perhaps you might care to reflect on a system that we take very much for granted: the organisation of pupils into classes by age-grouping. It is unlikely that you have ever stopped to consider why this particular form of grouping is appropriate. The questions in Task 6 may help you think the issue through.

Task 6 Reviewing age grouping

Imagine that you have to give a talk, to a group of teachers on an in-service course, explaining why it is appropriate that your school is organised by age-groups. Make notes for the talk. The headings supplied below are not exhaustive, but they may start you thinking.

- Insights from child development and psychology.
- Social importance of the peer-group.
- Ease of teaching.
- Overall advantages.

Mixed ability classes

Another form of grouping for learning which we take very much for granted is that of composing classes of children of a wide or full range of ability: mixed ability grouping as opposed to streaming. At the infant level this is rarely made into an issue, though there is active debate in most comprehensive schools. Of course, in small infant schools or departments, the small size of the intake may limit choice of organisation: a one-form entry cannot be streamed. But a two-form entry or above allows this possibility. So why precisely do most schools prefer to opt for a mixed ability approach even where mixed age groups are rejected? Below are some common reasons given by heads and teachers of infants.

- Grading children by ability is socially divisive.
- The infant school is too soon to make adequate judgements about pupils' academic potential.
- Children who are labelled as failures tend to fail, so this should be resisted.
- Streaming does not fit children to mix in ways commensurate with the real world.
- Children of varying abilities can learn to help or be helped by classmates.

If your class is mixed in ability you might find it instructive to review your own procedures with Task 7.

Task 7 Coping with a wide ability range

1   Set down the strategies you use to cope with the least able pupils.
2   List the ways in which you deal with the most able pupils.
3   From your own experience, list the advantages of mixed ability grouping.

In practice, though many infant schools or departments divide pupils into classes of mixed ability, once in those classes teachers employ methods of 'hidden streaming'. Thus, a mixed ability class may be divided for many purposes (numeracy, reading etc) into working groups. These may be given relatively fixed identities, often reinforced by names – red, blue, green; lions, tigers, bears. The underlying purpose of these groups is often to divide pupils into ability groups for key activities or particular academic elements of the curriculum. Mixed ability organisation is frequently no more than skin deep! This example does, however, make the point that school-level philosophies and methods of organisation may be modified quite radically within individual classrooms.

Grouping within the classroom

The commonest classroom groups are probably based upon friendship: children may well sit with their friends at tables of four, six or eight. These groups provide for social interaction. Classroom research with pupils of various age-groups suggests that the talk between individuals serves the function of keeping the group cohesive. Other interactions are task-based. Obviously, groups which chatter a lot and work little are less likely to produce effective learning in pupils. Part of the organisational skill of the teacher is to monitor output of work from groups and to be vigilant about time-wasting. Teachers need to tune in their observation and listening skills to keep track of the life of classroom groups. Task 8 may help you to watch groups more effectively.

Task 8 Observing classroom groups

Try to find an opportunity to watch classroom groups at work. You and a colleague might take it in turns to observe in one another's classroom. Over a period of about 20 minutes use each of the following measures of group activity. After the lesson, analyse the results and discuss the findings with your colleague.

1   Select one group of pupils and watch each pupil in turn for one minute. In each case, record how many seconds out of sixty the pupil is engaged on task, thus:-

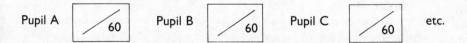

Express the results thus:

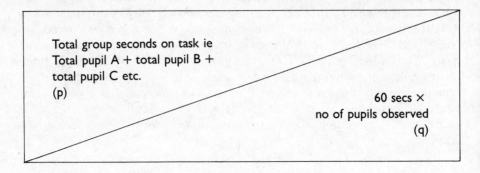

Total group seconds on task ie
Total pupil A + total pupil B +
total pupil C etc.
(p)

60 secs ×
no of pupils observed
(q)

So the percentage time spent on the task equals $\dfrac{p \times 100}{60 \times q}$ %

2   For five minutes observe the same group of pupils and record all interactions thus:

Pupil

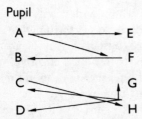

A ———————→ E
B ←——————— F
C
D
G
H

3   Eavesdrop on the conversation in the group for a further five minutes. Listen to each child's verbal contributions to the group's life. Categorise these contributions into those which are task-orientated (indicated by a plus sign) and those which distract others (indicated by a minus sign). Record the result thus:

Pupil A + + −   E −
      B +   F + − − +
      C − −   G +
      D nil   H − − −

4   Using the measures in 1, 2 and 3 above you should now be able to decide, with respect to your chosen group,
   ● the percentage time it spends on its task;
   ● the pattern of interactions, eg which pupils are isolates, which pupils are 'stars';
   ● which children are mainly task-orientated and which are more likely to distract others.

When you have thought through the issues about grouping for learning in this section of the book, have carried out the Tasks and considered their implications, you might like to answer each of the following questions in the context of your own teaching situation.

- What criteria of judgement should inform the choice of grouping method for a school/a classroom?
- How can a *variety* of grouping methods be employed to maximise learning of academic and social skills?
- How are your grouping methods affecting the education of the most and least able pupils in class?
- What principles of professional practice can you learn from close scrutiny of the life of groups in your classroom?

Unit 4

UNDERSTANDING SOCIAL RELATIONSHIP ISSUES

Children in Great Britain come to school a little before or immediately after reaching their fifth birthday; but they bring with them five years of extremely varied and variable experience received during one of the most formative segments of life. If we use the analogy of the child as clay in the hands of the potter, a good deal of moulding has gone on before the teaching profession gets the chance to shape the potential vessel!

The influence of background on young children

The reception teacher will do well to ponder on the factors that go to shape the lives of the youngsters who arrive on the first day of term. Here is just a selection of things which might constitute a checklist of factors that shape young lives – for better or worse:

1 Complete or disrupted family.
2 Relatively high or relatively low family income.
3 Good or poor housing conditions and facilities.
4 Large or small family.
5 Extended or nuclear family.
6 Affluent or impoverished neighbourhood.
7 Good or poor health of child or parents.

8   Genetic characteristics inherited from parents.
9   Father working or not employed.
10   Mother working or not employed.
11   Urban, suburban or rural environment.
12   Parents with good knowledge/little knowledge of education system.
13   Psychologically secure/insecure family climate.
14   Opportunities for peer-group social relationships available/lacking in the home.
15   Whether or not the child attended nursery school, playgroup etc.

There is good evidence to suggest that children's actual learning and learning potential at age five are adversely affected by at least some of those items appearing on the debit side of the above list (eg 1,2,3). Conversely, some of the items (such as 4,5,11) probably have more varied effects – good and bad – as they impinge on a child's development and educational progress. The most complete study of socio-economic factors on five-year-olds is undoubtedly to be found in Osborn, Butler and Morris (1984). Genetic factors are outside the control of society, but have a significant effect on the child's intellectual, emotional and physical school performance. The relative strength of genetic and social influences is a matter for debate: the short-hand term for this debate is the nature–nurture controversy. There are other factors at work in the environmental experience of young children – traumas at birth, for example, or the degree of maternal bonding which takes place in the first weeks of life – which almost certainly have lasting, important but usually immeasurable effects on progress.

Given that all this is so, then the teacher needs to be collector, interpreter and user of the data about the pupils in her care. The reception teacher especially needs a way of systematically keeping and recording information about her pupils which will enable her:

- to know the individual child intimately;
- to plan the best line of approach to his/her early learning experiences;
- to compensate for any deficiencies in background experience;
- to support and advise parents.

To this end she needs to develop a record-keeping system. At the same time she must be aware of her professional duties of confidentiality. It is best if records are anonymous and are always kept locked away and out of sight. (Consider, for example, the case of a teacher who leaves named records open and visible on a car seat in a playground where mothers congregate to collect their sons and daughters!)

Task 9 encourages you to develop your own record-keeping proforma.

Task 9 Keeping records about background data

1   Decide first of all on the *purposes* to which your collected information will be put (eg to inform yourself, your colleagues, parents, the headteacher, to spot problems or as an aide memoire).
2   From what *sources* will you be able to collect information: existing school records, parents, the pupils themselves?
3   Now decide what you need to know. Formulate this as a *list of headings*.
4   Now devise your proforma.
5   Your proforma can be trialled by attempting to complete it for one or two pupils. Make any necessary amendments. Now use it to gather data on all pupils.
6   Review the data to guide you into making the kinds of decisions which relate to your avowed purposes in 1 above.

Planning compensatory classroom experiences

If record-keeping can help the teacher to plan compensatory classroom activities, what kind of activities are likely to be required by pupils? They can probably be listed under main headings:
Social learning experiences
Emotional learning experiences
Sensori-motor experiences
Intellectual experiences
How can these be catered for in the infant school? Let us examine each in turn.

Social learning

Social learning takes place throughout the infant school and affects all aspects of its life. Indeed, the ethos of the school is critical in this form of education. Every day provides opportunities to learn: in school, in the classroom, in the dining hall, in the playground. Here are some typical learning opportunities for social skills:

*   entry to the classroom
*   conversation with the class teacher
*   talk with peers
*   running an errand to the school secretary
*   visiting the staffroom
*   taking part in a presentation for assembly
*   co-operative groupwork in the classroom
*   sharing toys on the patio
*   joining in playground games

- eating lunch
- buying at the school shop
- taking good work to the headteacher
- helping to tidy the classroom
- meeting visitors to the school
- seeing the school nurse

Emotional learning

Children learn to cope with emotions at two levels: through direct experience or by means of 'second-hand' knowledge.

Direct experience may involve such activities as

- looking after pets
- helping a neighbour
- being responsible for a classroom chore
- taking part in a play
- playing in the Home Corner

Indirect experience means learning, for example from stories told or read, how to cope in part with events which cannot take place in the classroom. So pupils may learn to cope with fear more easily through stories like 'The Wild Things', and the kinds of follow-up discussion a skilled teacher can encourage. This theme is taken up in more detail on page 34.

These activities may well help children to cope with crucial events: to understand the feeling of losing a treasured pet; to have confidence in front of a peer-group; to role play anger as 'mother' or 'father'.

It is crucial that young children learn to adapt to, or to control, their own emotions and also to see them in a positive light. Play is important in this respect and the effective teacher of young children will provide many opportunities for this, both in this context and that of the next heading.

Sensori-motor learning

Some children are deprived of proper development of sensori-motor skills. Perhaps they live in high rise flats where opportunities for physical play are limited. Some parents object to 'messy' activities such as water play; they may find it socially unacceptable to have the house untidy. For this reason, and to promote natural physical maturation, infant classrooms will have a sand tray and vessels for water play. There will also be toys: building blocks, Lego, jig-saw puzzles, things to ride on and in. There may be apparatus outdoors, too; a climbing frame, sand-pit, or a small adventure playground. Children like to imitate adults, so prams, wheelbarrows, spades and other larger toys allow practice of many physical skills. Balls and ropes, bean-bags and hoops are all grist to this mill. The major purpose here is not to learn skills in the systematic way that one might in a physical education session but to allow the child to experiment and to express himself or herself.

Intellectual experiences

A surprising number of children come from homes where intellectual pursuits are not commonplace. Television may substitute for reading. Parents do not read fluently, or are too busy, so there is no story-time in the home. Language skills are lacking in the parents and so children communicate monosyllabically, or use bad language, or have limited vocabularies, or pronounce words indistinctly or sloppily. Language deprivation may be worsened in immigrant communities. The child may be unused to seeing books in the house.

Compensatory education in these cases consists of two main factors: providing educational opportunities and encouraging positive attitudes. The opportunities consist of allowing children to wander off in quiet corners to look at books, to count coins or to listen to exciting stories told or read. Attitudes are communicated through the values shown to be accorded to these pursuits and to those who engage in them. Freedom and choice are probably crucial here.

Summary

Compensatory education can function effectively only after the teacher has got to know a child well and has probed the cause of any obvious problem. It does, of course, demand time and energy as well as professional judgement. The messages of this section of the book can be drawn together in the next Task.

 ## Task 10 Providing compensatory education

1 Look over the records you collected in Task 9. Choose three pupils whom you feel to have urgent but very different needs that can be satisfied in the classroom. (For example, you might select an only child who is unused to sharing, a child with a limited vocabulary, and one who needs help with keeping himself or herself clean and tidy.)

2 Plan some appropriate activities that you can give to each child to compensate for their current lack of experience.

3 Put these into practice discreetly in your classroom. Record and monitor the results in each case.

Individuals, boys and girls

Good classroom relationships between teacher and pupil or pupil and pupil depend to a large extent on sensible insights into the social issues underlying the education process. Each child needs to be seen as an individual with a personal value and a distinct identity. Teachers commonly do this through activities such as:

- knowing and always using names;
- commenting positively on children's dress;
- praising good work or behaviour;
- talking to the child about home, family;
- celebrating birthdays.

One aspect of classroom relationships often overlooked at this age is sex stereotyping. Research (May 1984) tends to suggest that even at the infant level some sex stereotypes are, perhaps unconsciously, promoted and even initiated by teachers. For example:

- Teachers may encourage boys to play with balls and spades, girls with dolls and skipping ropes.
- Teachers may organise seating to put like sexes together.
- Teachers may have fixed views (eg boys are more disruptive than girls) regardless of evidence.
- Teachers may allocate classroom chores on a gender basis – boys to carry, girls to tidy up.
- Classroom teaching materials may contain particular stereotypes.

The main battle here is to raise awareness of the issue. (We do not wish either to get bogged down in the debate, or to set out any viewpoint by way of propaganda). Task 11 may help to this declared end.

Task 11 Monitoring gender bias

1 Make an opportunity to observe your children at work and at play for a period of time.
2 Make notes on the friendship patterns, social contacts and the play activities of individual pupils.
3 Analyse your observations for stereotypes or gender bias as described in the text above.
4 If necessary, plan strategies to overcome any undesirable traits you discover.

Encountering parents

With young children, parents are very much part of the educational scene. Schools do, of course, vary in their policies towards parents. Some headteachers object to parents entering even infant schools without a formal appointment. Most pursue a more open, and more desirable, policy. In acting upon what follows you should be careful always to remain within the guidelines or conventions of your own school.

Whatever the policy towards parents in school, there will always be parents waiting at the school gate. For teachers of infants relationships with parents will usually be informal and contacts regular. This alone is reason enough for teachers to take seriously the nature of their accountability to parents. A major advantage of this daily encounter is that problems can be sorted out quickly. The teacher can say to mum: 'Sheila's a bit off-colour today; perhaps she should visit the doctor if she's no better tomorrow.' In return mum may well warn the teacher of a crisis in the family such as the death of a relative that may affect Johnny's work or behaviour for a week or two.

While this informal traffic in information is to be welcomed, there are more formal transactions, too. In many schools parents become quite deeply committed to school life. Some typical examples are listed below:

- parent managers
- parent committee members of the PTA
- parents helping on open evenings
- parents helping on school outings
- parents providing goods for a fete or party
- monthly assemblies open to parent visitors
- mothers attending with children for medicals
- parents invited to school plays or concerts
- parents helping in classrooms eg with cookery or craft

Occasionally a parent is 'difficult'. Such cases are rare – most are genuinely interested – but they do have the right to ask pertinent questions. If in doubt junior members of staff should always seek the head's advice. Student-teachers should not handle contact with parents alone.

The Task that follows should be carried out as a whole-school exercise rather than by an individual teacher.

Task 12 Devising a school policy towards parents

1   In the list of parental roles above, which currently apply in your school?
    What additional roles/contacts do parents of your children have with the school?

2   What are the existing school policies with respect to parents? Are they written down anywhere? Are they communicated to staff? To parents themselves?
3   How could the roles and contacts in 1 be improved and extended?
4   How can fathers be more closely involved in the life of the school?
5   Draw up a policy statement. If appropriate, include it in any documentation about the school which may be provided to parents of youngsters about to join the school.

Unit 5

LEARNING THROUGH PLAY

'Play.1. Move about in lively or unrestrained or capricious manner, frisk, flutter . . . Amuse oneself, sport, frolic, trifle, pass time pleasantly . . . be away from work . . . employ oneself in a game . . . '
(Concise Oxford Dictionary 1976 ed)

Taking two or three other dictionaries from your library shelves and looking up the word 'play', you would probably find similar implications of frivolity, inessentials and irrelevance. Contrast these with a scientist's use of the word when he or she says that young animals play. The implication here is rather more 'practise for life'. The same ambiguity surrounds the word in the infant school context.

 ## Task 13 Exploring the meaning of play

Test out this ambiguity by asking four or five colleagues or friends to define play and compare their answers with the dictionary definitions.

We have looked at two kinds of definition of play – frivolity and practice. But in an infant school context neither is exhaustive nor wholly appropriate.

It has been suggested that 'play is the highest level of child development. It is the spontaneous expression of thought and feeling . . . At this age, play is never trivial. It is serious and deeply significant.' (Froebel 1967)

Play must, on this view, be considered crucial to the child's emotional development, social development and motor skill development. The teacher cannot, therefore, treat it solely as a preparation for adult activities. Neither should she assume that free, unstructured play is the answer for natural development. Instead she needs to observe first, then direct, in order to encourage further investigation and logical thinking. Let us take an example:

The teacher provides challenging experiences for the children in water play. First she gives them plenty of time for free experimentation with a collection of items, some which will float and others which will sink. Then she steps in to direct a more particular activity. She extends the children's vocabulary as well as encouraging them to predict outcomes of experiments: eg if the milk bottle top floats on top of the water when it is laid flat with its edges turned slightly upwards, what will happen if it is crumpled up into a ball and laid on the water? (Montague 1979).

Task 14 Devising play activities

Try to devise a similar progression from free experimentation to a structured activity with *sand* play. Commercial apparatus and/or natural/classroom items may be incorporated into the chosen activity, eg funnels, water, paint pots.

Enriching play and encouraging development

A closer look at the development of the child's social skills, motor skills and emotional responses from age four to seven suggests a need for a careful balance between structured and unstructured play in the classroom and the playground.

The first consideration must be space. Children need 'somewhere' to play. Space facilitates movement and provides the opportunity for imaginative play. However, 'play can only take place in a non-threat situation. Only in such an environment can fantasy emerge and invention take place' (Van Der Eyken 1967). According to this study the children's favourite place to play was 'where nobody tells us off'. We have encountered similar preferences for total privacy in classroom experiments when the Home Corner was without the front panel (ie the section incorporating the windows and doors) for a few weeks. The children made makeshift 'walls' using net curtains across the opening to section off the area completely and played much more freely once they felt they were out of sight! The type of space for play need not remain constant in the classroom. Indeed, fantasy in play can be stimulated by a simple change in the Home Corner, for example. It could become an Indian tepee, an aquarium, a time machine or a monster's den. The possibilities are endless.

The teacher can also facilitate play of the kind described earlier, which imitates everyday life as the child encounters it. Children make observations and, later, like to imitate what they have seen. Piaget felt that a child pretending to telephone someone, then making her doll do the same, is evolving something which pleased her. Reproducing the action is a game which enables her to become more a part of her environment. He believed that in playing games like this, the child 'forms a vast network of devices which allow the ego to assimilate the whole of reality, ie to integrate it, in order to relive it, to dominate or to compensate for it' (in Beard R 1967).

Task 15 Observing play

When the opportunity for classroom observation arises, try to identify a few attempts by the children to make sense of their world by imitation. Any free play situation can be observed, for example, children playing with wooden bricks, a garage, model cars and a road plan (mat type).

Developing social skills through play

In this section we shall go on to explore how play takes its place in the development of social skills. We begin with a review of typical levels of development of children of four to five years and of six to seven years. You may find it helpful also to explore this issue in more detail by consulting a specialist text such as Gesell & Ilg *The First Five Years of Life* (1954).

Four-to-five-year-olds

Cries of, 'It's mine', 'He won't let me play', and 'I'm not playing any more' are very familiar to the teacher of reception and 'middle' infant children. Four- and five-year-olds seem to have no conception of sharing. In addition to helping the children to care about each other and to share out toys and opportunities fairly, the teacher needs to share out resources firmly, by the use of rules, often written out as signs on card in the classroom.

For example

> 4 children can play in
> the Home Corner

> Only 2 children can
> play in the sand

> There is room for 6
> children at the painting
> table.

Maximum numbers really do need to be stated or 'free play' very quickly becomes a 'free-for-all'!!

Four-year-olds can understand the need for 'taking turns', despite their generally self-willed behaviour. Groups of children playing together, for example, at the sand tray, should be changed at quite frequent intervals, as four-year-olds tend to be alternately aggressive and co-operative with each other, as they are with adults. This age group really enjoys strongly dramatic play and dressing up, and their natural curiosity and ability to ask questions endlessly make play provision obvious. Free play in the Home Corner and free experimentation with sand and water are very valuable opportunities for four-year-olds to develop their social sense.

As children reach the age of five (and remember, one can only generalise on issues like these), they tend to prefer to play in groups of two and seldom in groups of more than five. There is very little solitary or parallel play; although imaginative play may give the *appearance* of co-operation, in fact it involves very little. Each child plays to his own ends with little concern for the group. Five-year-olds tend to be able to play well together if the group is small, although pairs of friends may be shifting. In unsupervised play, some can be very 'bossy', or play roughly, or cry very easily. In fact, at this age children generally prefer to have an adult nearby.

Let us pause, then, in this review of social development through play to apply some of the messages to the classroom.

Task 16 Devising a structured play activity for four- to five-year-olds

Consider all the points raised above with regard to five-year-olds' social behaviour. In the light of these, devise one structured play activity which would be suitable for a small group (state the number of children) for a given period of time. Put your plan into operation. Observe and record what happens. To what extent does it confirm what has been said? What new insights have you gained?

Six-year-olds

A group of six-year-olds can play well together, but each wants his or her own way. Grouping is very flexible; one child could leave unnoticed. Yet children of this age are interested in having friends. Some constant friendships begin to develop at this age, although even in these relatively stable relationships play is continually interrupted by arguments. The teacher needs to be careful not to group friends together for every activity in the classroom for this reason.

Six-year-olds are extremely keen to win prizes and will respond well to rewards and praise. Unfortunately their desire to win often leads to cheating in some games, which again leads to arguments. The teacher needs to monitor any game very carefully. Some teachers are opposed to any element of competition on social or philosophical grounds. Such a view fails to reflect reality and may not be in the child's long-term interests.

By the time the child reaches seven he is learning to cope with the experience of losing, but he or she must also experience success. In group play, each child tends to be concerned only for his own individual ends and often several children 'gang up' on one other child, who in turn, may worry about his place in the group, and within the class. The teacher needs to recognise this when it occurs, and to facilitate situations in which the child feels valued and the other children realise that he too is an important member of the class. The child could perhaps take on the highly valued post as class shop-keeper for the morning (in a structured play situation), playing with a group of children with whom he gets on well.

TABLE 5 Developing motor skills

A checklist for the teacher of four- to seven-year-olds

Ability/Development	Provision
Four-year-olds	
Turns sharp corners, running, pushing, pulling.	Free play in playground where space available. Limit movement eg in school hall (in PE) where space is restricted.
Climbs ladders. Walks upstairs and down, one foot per step. Can run on tiptoe. on tiptoe. Hops on one foot.	Free choice of large apparatus in PE (climbing frame, boxes, ladders etc).
Fine movements Builds three steps with six cubes after demonstration.	Any constructional toys to copy after demonstration or picture of finished item to copy. Eg Lego, sticklebricks, connector bricks, octons, constructo-straws, Figure Craft.
Draws man with head and legs, possibly trunk or features.	Free painting/drawing.

Ability/Development	Provision
Five-year-olds	
Greater ease and control of general bodily activity. Control over large muscles more advanced than small.	Tasks set in PE in floor work can be continued on the large apparatus. For example: 'curling and stretching', 'transference of body weight'.
Active and skilful in climbing, swinging, sliding. Runs lightly on toes. Alternate feet descending stairs.	
Fine movements	
Draws recognisable human.	Free painting/drawing.
Likes to colour within lines, to cut and paste simple things but is not adept.	Simple collage.
Six-year-olds	
Very active, in almost constant motion. Tries stunts on bars. Plays active games with singing. Skips to music.	Direction can be given in movement lessons to channel activity. Movement tasks in PE could include varying levels, in floor work and on apparatus.
Fine movements	
Often awkward and clumsy in manipulation (with buttons, laces). Cuts and pastes paper.	Enjoyment and some success could be provided by dressing and undressing dolls or assembling constructional toys.
Able to use pencils properly.	Correct letter formation practice in sand with finger, then with paint and finger, then with pencil on paper.
Seven-year-olds	
Shows more caution in many gross motor activities.	Adventure playground activities in a controlled environment.
Activity variable, sometimes very active, sometimes inactive. Repeats performance persistently. Has crazes for certain activities eg roller skating.	Opportunities to pursue current enthusiasms.
Fine movements	
Manipulation of tools more tense but more persistence shown.	New experiences eg woodwork, photography.

Developing emotional responses through play

The reception teacher will often hear 'No', 'I won't', 'I'll do it this way, not like you said', or similar defiant remarks from the four-year-old new-starter. This is partly due to fear or insecurity: the child doesn't like to admit inability, but is less sensitive to praise or blame than a three-year-old and so is less prepared simply to conform. Mindless conformity is undesirable, but the teacher does need to keep the classroom works oiled. How can the teacher deal with this?

Task 17 Dealing with defiance

Think back over your classroom behaviour or observe a colleague at work. Note any examples of children failing to co-operate with the teacher. How does she handle the situation? Make a list of possible and/or observed strategies.

At four, children may have other fears, too. The dark; wild animals; 'monsters'; witches. *Fantasy and reality run into each other*. Often, as teachers, we seem to encourage it – story time can transport children into haunted houses, dark leafy jungles and so on. The teacher should take care to explain the difference between the real world and the world of fantasy. Where possible, fears from the real world can be dispelled by the provision of first- or second-hand experiences.

For example, animals could be brought into school for a 'Pets' Day' to allay fears of certain species! Class pets are always invaluable in this way, and for helping the children to realise the care which is needed in handling any living creature (see Unit 9). In terms of second-hand experiences, a story can often help to lessen fears by drawing pictures in the child's mind as he listens, as 'The owl who was afraid of the dark' would, for instance.

The five-year-olds in an infant class will still have their fears, but they manifest themselves mainly at night-time. In school hours, the five-year-olds are largely able to be helpful and even co-operative. They tend to be quite protective towards the younger members of the class if it is family grouped. Problems occur when the older children feel they should have priority over the younger members of the class – eg always wanting to take the role of the 'mother' or the 'father' in playing 'House' whilst the younger children play 'the baby'. Or taking the role of 'the teacher' or the 'headteacher' whilst playing 'school', the younger children playing the pupils.

In this situation, the teacher could set up a semi-structured play activity giving the children roles to play with themes to provide guidelines:

• You are giving a birthday party for your grandmother . . . each of the family is to make preparations. (Family gets busy, one making a cake, another tidying up the 'house' etc).

- You have all been invited to a wedding. Where are the bride and groom? Here they are . . . you will all need to dress up for the occasion. (All the children find clothes from dressing up box).

At six, there seems to be more marked disequilibrium between one child and another. Six-year-olds are highly emotional; there is a tendency for extremes of behaviour, very good or very bad! Fortunately the teacher may capitalise on the good behaviour when it occurs with a great deal of praise and approval in any of the child's activities as this age group really does enjoy praise and approval.

Seven is more a 'feeling' age. At this age the children play much more happily together, and are more considerate towards each other. They can be left to work out a theme in dramatic play for themselves. They will only become angry with themselves if they feel they cannot perform well and achieve the high goals they have set. Although less aggressive than they were at five or six, they often threaten to 'beat someone up', and do sometimes fight. Verbal objection comes to the fore with this age group with the plaintive cry of 'It isn't fair!' All the earlier principles of firmness and consistency apply at this end of the school.

In this overview of play we have seen how this aspect of classroom work is important, not only for learning but for the healthy development of the self-image of the child and for the proper integration of the individual into his or her expanding world. To conclude this section you might like to try Task 18.

Task 18 Reviewing learning through play

Make the opportunity to watch a group of children at play in the playground, in a park or at home. Try to assess what learning is taking place. Generate some headings to classify this learning, eg social learning, motor experience etc. Apply the understanding you have gained from this Task to your observations in the classroom and the experiences you provide there for pupils.

Unit 6

PROMOTING READING & PRE-READING SKILLS

Reading readiness

Theories of reading readiness emerged from the interest in child development and the study of abilities. It emerged that all children were not equally equipped to carry out a given learning task at any one particular age. It was also realised that children do not receive the same types of stimulus in their different home or neighbourhood environments, have varying levels of innate ability to learn and consequently develop at different rates.

This led to the idea that, at the point at which children start school (at age four or five), some children would be 'ready' to begin reading while others would not. The only problem was the determination of which children were 'ready' and which children were not!

Due to the fact that developmental psychology saw the development of the child as a 'gradual unfolding of the latent powers within' (Moyle 1968), theory held that the moment of readiness was determined by maturation, and should not be 'helped along'. Theoretically, the child would pick up a book to read when he was ready. Every teacher can think of an example of a child who found no problems with learning to read yet who, before he was asked by the teacher to begin reading, had never showed any inclination to do so.

These early theories claimed that to attempt to speed up readiness resulted in feelings of failure in the child and hence created emotional problems. Obviously failure could result if appropriate pre-reading exercises and experiences were not made available to the child. Young children sometimes have difficulty understanding the 'technical' terms – 'letter', 'word' and 'sound'. Piaget described children's language even up to the age of eight as egocentric, and Vygotsky claimed that it was precisely the abstract quality of language which proved a barrier to young children's learning of skills like reading (Horner 1984). However, while it was once fashionable to believe that children should not learn to read until they had reached a mental age of six years six months on a test such as Schonell, no one would now seriously claim that pre-reading and reading activities should be so delayed. It is, of course, proven that a child can learn to read at an advanced level well before he reached a mental age of six-and-a-half years. Evidence has suggested that a mental age of two-and-a-half to three-and-a-half years is sufficient for the learning of words without 'ill effects', if environmental factors are favourable.

But this success in reading, and the readiness for learning to read initially, are dependent upon several factors which can be grouped as follows:

- *Pyschological*: such as normal growth and maturation, auditory and visual acuteness and the correct functioning of speech organs.
- *Environmental*: such as the linguistic background and social experiences of the child.
- *Emotional*: such as personality traits and motivation towards reading.
- *Intellectual*: such as general intellectual ability, visual and auditory dis- crimination, and problem-solving abilities relating to language.

As far as the teacher is concerned, that innate capacity for learning, the child's maturation, parental preparations for reading, and the experiences the child has had as a result of his particular background, may be out of her control. But emotional and intellectual factors in school time are not, so the child's motivation towards reading can be encouraged; visual discrimination can be developed; and activities can be devised which can help the child improve his problem-solving abilities. Some strategies a teacher can adopt to help the child towards readiness include the following.

- Associating reading with pleasure through sharing well-illustrated, well- written story books with the children.
- Showing the children what 'reading' actually means – showing them the words which tell about the pictures.
- Showing the children that words contain letters and each has a sound.
- Illustrating that one begins at the top and moves down the page.
- Showing the movement across the page from left to right.
- Providing the children with tasks which develop an understanding of the above, eg letter and word discrimination exercises, left/right orientation exercises etc.

In planning further activities the teacher might look to a list of skills and abilities which need to be mastered before a child is ready to learn to read.

But lists of this nature can make too much of a distinction between a stage of 'preparation' and real reading. What the teacher needs most is a guide to show which level of achievement a child has reached and suggestions for activities which will take him to the next level. Moyle (1968) produced such a guide which tried to identify stages in reading readiness. Table 6 is based in part upon Moyle's work. Note that a checklist like the one illustrated in the Table should be tried every few weeks when exploring an individual's readiness. However, it is not necessary for all answers to be affirmative before *pre*-reading begins. The checklist may itself alert the teacher to the necessity for remedial action on some issues (eg sight, hearing). Obviously the Table is a guide only, and the teacher must ultimately both adapt it to her needs and use it with discrimination.

TABLE 6 A checklist for reading readiness

Child's name _____
Date of birth _____
Date of entry to school _____
Date of observations _____

Physical readiness

Is vision normal?	YES	NO
Is hearing normal?	YES	NO
Is articulation/pronunciation clear?	YES	NO
Is pronunciation free from gross errors?	YES	NO
Can the child use scissors/tools etc?	YES	NO
Can he/she use a pencil/felt tip?	YES	NO
Is he/she normally fit and energetic?	YES	NO

Psychological readiness

Does he/she show interest in language?	YES	NO
Does he/she express him/herself clearly?	YES	NO
Is vocabulary suited to the reading materials which will be available for use?	YES	NO
Does he/she enjoy story time?	YES	NO
Does he/she play normally for his/her age?	YES	NO
Does he/she represent ideas in drawings?	YES	NO
Does he/she memorise short passages?	YES	NO
Does he/she concentrate on a task effectively?	YES	NO
Can he/she view items in order from left to right?	YES	NO
Can he/she interpret pictures?	YES	NO
Can he/she predict possible outcomes eg for a story?	YES	NO
Does he/she make connections between printed symbols and the spoken word?	YES	NO

Social and emotional readiness

Does he/she work well with other children?	YES	NO
Does he/she listen to others?	YES	NO
Does he/she work alone satisfactorily?	YES	NO
Does he/she take reasonable care of materials?	YES	NO
Does he/she usually complete set tasks?	YES	NO
Does he/she co-operate readily with adults?	YES	NO

Task 19 Assessing reading readiness

Consider the approach to the teaching of reading which you employ (either as a matter of personal choice or to comply with your school's policy).

Keep in mind the resources and materials used in your approach. Now look over the checklist in Table 6 and add to the list of headings anything which you think may be appropriate for the child to achieve before he starts to learn to read by your method.

Pre-reading

Reading skills are seen by teachers, and of course by parents, as central to a child's learning at this age. But it would be wrong to treat reading skills wholly in isolation from other language performance. The situation is summed up very simply in Table 7 below, and language itself is discussed in Unit 8. Table 7 indicates links between aspects of language, and at the infant level these links need to be reinforced continually. It is here, indeed, that a language policy at school level begins. The teacher needs to be *conscious* of the policy because, at five, children think *through* language, and *with* language; but they don't think *about* language.

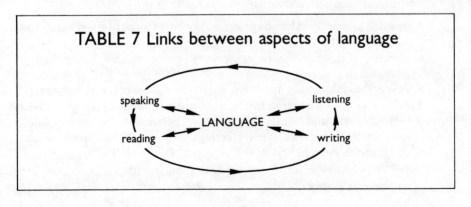

TABLE 7 Links between aspects of language

speaking   listening

LANGUAGE

reading   writing

Fostering an awareness of spoken language

Children are often unaware of how they are *using* the language they speak. They need to learn how to *listen* in new ways and to *talk* about what they are *hearing*. The teacher needs to explore the extent of children's listening and language awareness, and their abilities to communicate about things heard (or seen). Since TV plays such a large part in many children's lives this might be a good place to start.

Task 20 Exploring children's listening and speaking

Ask the children which television programmes they watch. Make a bar-chart to explore the most popular programmes. Ask individuals to explain which are their most or least favourite programmes and to say why.

What is likely to emerge from Task 20 is that most youngsters view television programmes for entertainment but, more importantly, they view in an unstructured way. Many children will put cartoons high on their list of preferences, but often these are comparatively wordless. By contrast, using a television programme as a teaching aid in school demands quite sophisticated language appreciation.

Watching, listening and discussing effectively are important study skills in today's classrooms and these skills have to be taught as part of an early language programme. The language facility and interest generated will lead on to the desire and readiness for reading.

Here are some things which a teacher can do to make school television a more effective language and learning experience.

1   Viewing should always have a purpose. Tell the children beforehand what the purpose is to be.

2   When watching a school broadcast, entertaining presentation is obviously desirable to sustain the children's interest; but ensure that the children's attention is focused on different points made in the programme by

- suitable preparation for the programme; an introduction – what to look for, listen for, etc;
- directing their attention to particular items of interest during the programme;
- asking the children about specific points mentioned in the programme;
- following up the programme by asking the children to reflect on what they have seen and heard. They might speculate about what they would have done if they had been a certain character in the story, or in a programme such as BBC1's 'Words and Pictures'. The teacher could ask the children to think of words beginning with 'ch', using the programme as a springboard.

Encouraging recognition of words as separate units

The children need to come to understand that when they speak, they use *separate words*. They need to be conscious of where words *begin* and *end*. Games such as 'I Spy' would be impossible without this understanding.

Outlined below is a classroom game which helps to promote understanding of words as separate units (Reed & Donaldson 1979).

The Counters Game

Each child is given a sheet of paper complete with a numbered grid which has four spaces per line.

1			
2			
3			

The children need to place a counter in the spaces each time the teacher says a word. Begin with children's names (*not* the names of the children playing the game). The children repeat the names and place a counter on a space each time. Once accomplished in this they could be encouraged to 'think' the words and place the counters.

After names, the teacher could use simple one or two syllable words like table, dog, carpet, bird, apple.

Followed by actual sentences –

We like playing.
Run along the street.

Later on the teacher could use more complicated words with several syllables such as 'holiday'.

Task 21 Devising a language game

Devise a simple game of your own to establish the understanding of words as separate units. Try out the game in your own classroom.

Defining the uses of writing

As they progress in their use and awareness of language, children need to understand why writing is necessary. They need to realise that it *represents the words we speak* and thus carries meaning. This is *not obvious*. A focus on how the writing system works is also necessary - eg that it reads from left to right etc.

Once again, games can aid understanding of the uses of writing. For example, the Magician Game (Reed and Donaldson, 1979):

> The 'Magician' could be an older child from another class, an NNEB member of staff, or NNEB student. This person leaves the room whilst the teacher hides an object chosen by the children. The teacher then writes on the board the object and where it is hidden. The magician is then recalled and asked 'What have we hidden and where have we hidden it?'
>
> After an obvious look at the board, the magician provides the name and position of the object. The exercise is repeated once or twice. Then the teacher asks the children – 'Do you know how the magician knew?' 'Do you know the magic secret?' 'Do you think anyone told him?'

Task 22 Exploring the uses of writing

Devise a simple exercise to try out on reception age children (perhaps a colleague could help if your own class's age range is not appropriate). The exercise ought to illustrate one use of writing.

Capitalising on everyday occurrences

An effective teacher needs to use every opportunity as it arises to illustrate uses of writing; for example, the children are often asked to take home letters giving their parents information. Explain to the children how the letter will inform people about particular items of interest where word of mouth would not be sufficient. Messages are often forgotten, whereas writing is something concrete, a reminder. Often essential, too.

- How else could a postman deliver letters?
- Without a written shopping list how could people remember all they needed from the supermarket?
- Without a written warning on bleach or medicine bottles, how would we know they could be dangerous?

Therefore we *need* writing.

Here are some things you can do to help the children grasp this particular message:

1   Get the children to differentiate between writing and pictures by colouring the pictures and putting a ring round the writing.
2   Make a collection of things the children can find from home which include words and captions eg labels.
3   Stage a 'Name Hunt'. Hide the children's name cards around the classroom and ask them to find the word which is their own name.
4   Play the 'Caterpillar Game': 'Children beginning to write and read show a marked tendency to recognise the letters of their own name in a variety of print styles' (Dewhurst 1985). Using different styles of print, provide the children with several caterpillar boards to which they match the first letter of their name. Thus A is A whether it is written 'A', 'a', '**A**' etc.

'CATERPILLAR GAME'

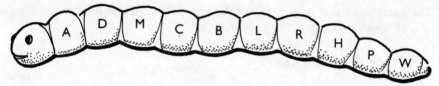

Promoting awareness of words as separate letters

Letter recognition and letter formation are vital. A 'Synchrofax' machine 'Phonic Alphabet' sheet is one aid which provides practice in both.

The teacher needs to begin to focus on words as separate letters as well as to focus on words themselves as outlined previously (p41).

A useful linking exercise using familiar words might be:

Hickory Dickory Dock | 3 |

The mouse ran up the clock | 6 |
etc

This could be followed by Reed & Donaldson's (1979) 'Letter Links':

hen | 3 |

Followed by identification of first and last letters
eg

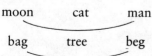

moon   cat   man

bag   tree   beg

One of the most difficult and most necessary skills for reading stems from the awareness that words are 'joined-up sets of sounds'. Developing such awareness involves some phonics teaching, but it need not involve simply phonics 'drill'. Once again, games have their part to play, for example: 'I went for a walk and I saw a d.o.g' (sounded out for the children). Examples are legion and you can make up your own.

Developing specific skills necessary for reading

To begin to read effectively a child will need to be reasonably efficient in five areas of skill

- Auditory discrimination
- Visual discrimination
- Hand/eye co-ordination
- Discrimination of letter shapes and sounds
- Memory

The paragraphs that follow look at these skills in turn and suggest a few ways in which you might begin to reinforce them.

Auditory discrimination

The children need both to *interpret* and to *use* the sounds they hear.

Task 23 Promoting auditory discrimination

Make your own tape of sounds: a telephone ringing, whistling, a knock on the door, a lawn mower at work, birds singing. Use the tape
either as a classroom game to test the general abilities of the children
  or with individual children as a guide to their specific skills and reading readiness.

Visual discrimination

Some possible ways to promote visual discrimination – essential as a first in word recognition – include

- Recognition of similarities and differences
- Completion of unfinished pictures
- Reversal identification (eg ▭ ▭ ▭ ▭)
- Matching (eg shape to shape, object to object)
- Mistake identification (eg cars with one wheel missing)
- Tracing journeys (eg bee to hive)
- Pattern completion

Some ideas for exploring similarities and differences are listed in Table 8. You should also tackle Task 24.

TABLE 8 Exploring similarities and differences

1   At the simplest level match colour to colour, shape to shape; spot differences in colour, shape etc.

2   Classifying – 'allows children to practise and promote the skills of comparison and differentiation, of deduction and elimination.' (ILEA 1976) Begin with apparatus for sorting, followed by use of picture cards. It is essential to allow time for sorting and discussion. The teacher's role is vital for the extension and clarification of the children's language. When the children are familiar with the cards, a variety of games can be played.

3   Pelmanism – all cards are spread face down. Each child turns over 2 cards. If they both belong to the same group, which must be named, the child keeps the cards.

4   Snap – the name of the group (eg 'tigers', 'diamonds') should be called out – not simply 'snap'.

5   Happy families – first get children to collect one family. Later to collect two or three each.

Task 24 Collecting aural and visual discrimination games

Capitalise on the suggestions made above in the paragraphs about aural and visual discrimination to begin to build up your own resource collection of discrimination games for your classroom. Have the games readily available and encourage children to use them in spare moments.

Hand/eye co-ordination

This can be developed, for example, through:

- pattern–making with fingers and/or brushes with paint and in sand
- 'colour-in' shapes
- use of templates and own hands and feet to draw round
- tracing over a pattern with a pencil or finger – writing patterns
- following a line which is 'entangled' with another, eg balloon strings

Many classroom activities require these skills, so watch for opportunities to practise them *at all times*, not just when pre-reading is the uppermost consideration or goal.

Letter shapes and sounds

You may care to add your own ideas to the following, which will serve as a stimulus to your thinking:

- Provide pictures of eg animals with the same initial sound. The children have to identify the odd one out. Which begins with a different letter?
- Provide pictures with words in caption form. The child has to complete the word by supplying the missing first letter.
- As above, but the child inserts the missing letter from a selection.

Memory

A key-note here is practice, and the alert teacher can use a multiplicity of opportunities, as well as create them. Again, here are a few suggestions to start you thinking:

- Encouraging recall   of television programmes
  of places visited
  of events in the child's life
  of stories told in class

- A contrived activity such as Kim's game:

  The children look at a collection of items on a tray for, say, one minute. Then they close their eyes. The teacher removes one item, and the children are asked to open their eyes and identify which.

Summary comments on pre-reading activities

The infant classroom is a busy environment and much of what goes on there can be used to promote and assess reading readiness and pre-reading skill. Table 9 augments the ideas given above. For a description of a teacher's approach to pre-reading you might also care to look at Kerry (1986) pages 58–62. For the psychological underpinning of reading skill you might consult Kennedy (1984). Fundamentally, of course, the child must *want* to learn to read; and the part played by stories, story-telling and books both at school and in the home is crucial. This is sufficiently self-evident not to need labouring in a workbook of this kind: but the theme is picked up in Table 9.

TABLE 9 A checklist of activities and skills relating to pre-reading

Vocabulary enrichment
- Story telling.
- Story reading.
- Creating a warm and exciting story-time on a regular basis.
- Repetition of old favourites.
- Providing stories well within the children's capabilities.
- Providing some stories about situations beyond the child's experience but with points of contact for the child to grasp.
- Using poems and rhymes to allow the children to play with sounds and enjoy them.
- News and talking time when the children can talk freely either to the class or in a small group.
- Discussing pictures in the classroom and drawings made by the children.
- Home play.

Labels and captions, books and print
- Providing books of all kinds: picture books, books with a few words to each picture, books with a simple repetitive story previously read by the teacher, scrap-books, class picture books etc.
- Labelling a picture, telling a story in one or two sentences.
- Displaying wall stories in the classroom.
- Using the child's own name: on name cards, pictures, coat peg etc.
- Everything has a name – using nouns, labels for parts of the room, shop, house, door, window, craft table etc.
- Making job lists – for straws for milk, feeding class pets etc.

In fact, *almost any activity which encourages the child to observe is a pre-reading activity.*

An approach to reading

'The way children are taught to read tells them what adults think literacy is.' (Meek 1982).

Contemporary research findings into early development of reading have been interpreted by many teachers as criticisms of much of their current practice. The problem to be solved seems to be: what else could replace the tried and tested methods such as sentence method, 'look and say', 'whole word' and phonic methods? In many schools, the Language Experience Approach (LEA) has been employed as an alternative and quite often in combination with the more traditional methods.

The advantages of the LEA method are that it 'emphasises the need of the learner to see what speech looks like in writing . . . It is based on what the learner already knows rather than what he or she does not know. It can work with published resources (eg 'Breakthrough to Literacy', Longman) or with teacher-made materials.' (Moon 1985).

It should be noted that this method is also easily adapted for use with computers – concept boards plugged into micros mean that text can be created from individual word banks.

Consequently teachers need to find an approach which best matches their own understanding, their children and their school. In the simplified view of reading in Table 10 it can be seen that a variety of methods can be employed simultaneously. For example:

'Written material from everyday situations written by the children' – LEA
'Labels in the classroom' – Look and Say method
'Letters and their sounds' – Phonics

All these methods can be quite naturally combined together to form a cohesive reading scheme with additional use of well-chosen published 'readers'.

Interest could even be stimulated in the early stages by use of the Sentence Method; simple pictures with equally simple stories beneath them, class news books, individual news books, labels on classroom walls and children's own pictures. These could be read frequently by the class, group or individual. Later, quick flash cards may be used so that the child recognises the reading matter apart from the picture.

Simple class reading or story books can be made and used at this stage, stories based on the child's own interests – his own day, going to school, a visit to the seaside, park, supermarket etc – the pictures being drawn, painted or crayonned by the teacher or children and the story added by the teacher.

Flashcards for the first 'reader' in a scheme could be introduced next and letter sounds taught, see Table 11.

As the children are ready, three-letter word building and blending should be taught eg ca-n, ca-t. Then c-at, b-at. This should be followed by the teaching of letter combinations as they occur in the readers eg th, sh, etc and vowel blendings eg oo, ou etc.

Picture books also have a vital part to play and can be used together with books specially packaged as reading schemes. Authors such as Pat Hutchins, John Burningham, and Ron Maris for example have proved that children can read and understand and enjoy picture books and respond to them at a more 'affective' level. Children refer to them as 'real' books!

Recent developments in the concept of 'shared reading', along with the belief that 'children learn to read by reading' and do this best when reading 'real'

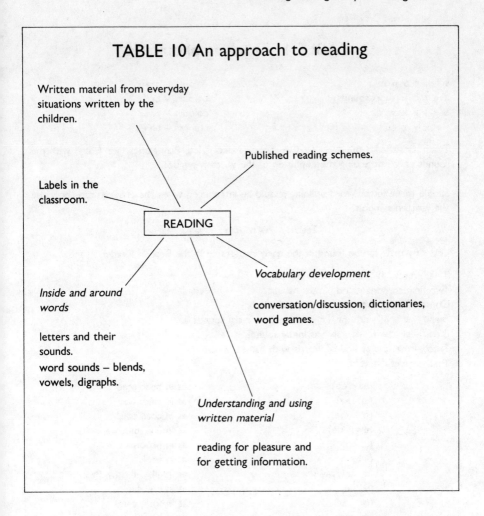

TABLE 10 An approach to reading

Written material from everyday situations written by the children.

Published reading schemes.

Labels in the classroom.

READING

Vocabulary development

conversation/discussion, dictionaries, word games.

Inside and around words

letters and their sounds.
word sounds – blends, vowels, digraphs.

Understanding and using written material

reading for pleasure and for getting information.

books, have led to many schools abandoning the more traditional reading scheme. Instead we see a new style of readers such as *Story Chest* (Wheaton 1984), which has a format like that of a conventional story book. Some schools have gone so far as to use only 'real' books of this nature.

Another advantage of this approach is that shared reading books such as *Read Together* (Story Chest 1986) or *Big Books* (Ginn, Reading 360) allow the teacher to read stories with the children. In the process, which as we have seen is an enjoyable one for youngsters, the teacher points to the words as she reads, and indicates left and right movement and top and bottom movement. The stories are couched in language which is immediately appropriate to the children. After a couple of reads the children are asked to join in.

TABLE 11 Teaching phonics

s f h t p n m r	colours – green
a e i o u (short sounds)	colours – buff
b c l g k w d	colours – pink
j v x y z qu	colours – blue

Teach these from the early days in school. Make it fun. Play games like 'I Spy' with the sounds only, not adding the confusion of the written symbol.

Simple three letter word building should be introduced when the children can recognise the written symbols.

Teach: fa - n   fan   fa - t   fat

Lists of words can be found in the early readers or in the Beacon Reading Manual.

ll   ss   mm   ff   nn   need to be taught.
Two final consonants nd   mp   nt   st
Consonant digraphs sh   nk   ng   ck   tch
Blend – sn   pl   dr   pr   cr   cl   etc as initial sounds.
Blend – ch   wh   th   sh   as initial sounds.
Teach – magic e at end of words with names of vowels.
Teach vowel digraphs.

(ea ee)	as in near, tree
(ai ay)	as in paid, way
(oa oe)	as in coal, toe
(ew ue)	as in few, blue
(oo)	as in broom
(oo)	as in took
(a au aw)	as in all, call, saw, Paul
(y ie)	as in my, die
(or ar)	as in fork, car
(er ir ur)	as in her, sir, purr
(y ey)	as in dolly, chimney
(le)	as in little, bubble
(ou ow)	as in found, cow
(oi oy)	as in oil, boy
(igh)	as in light

c before e prounced s   as in ice, face
ph   as in phone.
ing, ink,   as in wing, blink.
silent letters   as in limb, knot, wrap, often, half, gnat.
tion, sion,   as in attention, procession

The teacher pays special attention to 'heavy duty' words (the, said, and etc). This method emphasises that the children will read through *wanting* to read.

Opportunities should also be provided for the children to read independently, browse and look at books. They should also be allowed to take books home. Parents should be encouraged to share books with their children.

Involving parents

Parents and family can play a vital role in the school reading programme. In particular teachers should note the sound advice from the Centre for the Teach- of Reading (1984):

> 'Designating parents to the task of raising money or covering books should surely be balanced with other activities specifically concerned with their own child.'

The same publication suggests three possible ways of involving parents.

- Set up a pre-school library to entice toddlers and parents into school.
- Provide parents with specific guidelines about how to hear their children read at home.
- Establish a school book-shop to help parents select appropriate reading material for their children.

There are many others and you may care to add your own to this list. To conclude this section, and to help clarify your own thinking, you might like crystallise your thoughts by trying to complete Task 25.

Task 25 Formulating a reading policy

You have been given the task of writing to parents to explain how you tackle pre-reading skills (or the teaching of reading if your class is older), and to set out unambiguously what they can do to help. Compose an appropriate letter of about one-and-a-half A4 sides of typescript.

Listening to reading

'Reading aloud: make it worth doing'

Most teachers (Thomas 1982) believe that it is essential to the effective progress of the child for them to listen to the child reading. It can be made into a more pleasurable experience for the child in several ways, by:

- Creating an environment which displays books in attractive ways, and ensuring that there are well-illustrated and well-written story books avail- able; talking about the books and displays.

- Allowing the children to read aloud books they have chosen from the selection, ones they are attracted to and will enjoy.
- Placing cassette tapes and accompanying books in the book corner so that children come to value stories read aloud.
- Allowing the children to take books home to read to parents.
- Reading aloud to the children as much as possible.

 ## Task 26 Listening to reading

Try to think of at least two other strategies you could employ to encourage the children to enjoy reading aloud.

'Come and read to me'

At reading time, the teacher ought to ensure that her attention will not be distracted for at least five minutes while she listens to the child read. She needs to give the rest of the class some work which will keep them occupied for at least that length of time and to establish precedents about not interrupting. The teacher also needs to sit where she can see the rest of the class and be aware of what they are doing in an unobtrusive way. When hearing a child read:

- Begin with pleasant remarks to the child and smile to help establish the one-to-one relationship. Recap the last page: 'What happened here?' Revise any words which may have been a problem last time.
- Make connections with the story-line and the child's own experience: 'Have you ever done that, been there, seen this?'
- Check to see whether the child is over-reliant on pictures or if he has mastered word attack skills.
- Allow the use of a card marker to slide down the pages, it helps to focus attention on one line at a time.
- If the child miscues, try waiting at first. Only if he still cannot read the word, go back to the beginning of the sentence. If he still cannot read the word, encourage word attack skills eg
  What does the word begin with? or
  What does the word end with? or
  What sound is in the middle?
  Should none of these strategies work it may be more effective to tell the child the correct answer and move on.
- Now and again, back-track and use re-reading of a passage to encourage fluency and intonation.
- Ask at least one comprehension question, or try to link it with his own personal experience.

- Find something to praise.
- Record the child's progress.
- End as you began, with a smile and pleasant remark.

Recording errors

Individual progress is easily tracked if the teacher adopts a short-hand system for recording errors in her own notes on the children. The symbols below are very useful for this, and give the teacher an idea of areas where the child needs help. You could of course, make up your own shorthand system.

Error	Symbol
substitution	cat^(kitten)
omission	○
non-response	cat / R̄
repetition	R̄
correction	⌒c
insertion	∧ on

Typical problems

Goodman (1970) suggested that the errors children made when they read aloud should be treated as miscues, because they are picking up certain cues in the reading situation and have made a poor guess in the light of their expectations and ideas about what the situation involves. Their cues are related to the extent of their knowledge about letters and their sounds, the order of words in a sentence and the importance of word endings, the meaning of words and the look of words. The teacher has to decide if the child's miscues show an effort to produce a word which is a 'good fit' in relation to a number of these clues or if he is at a stage whereby he is only able to consider one type of 'clue' and cannot check how good a guess he has made. Moon (1980) provides a useful list of miscues, possible causes and possible intervention strategies for the teacher. This list is included here as Table 12.

Sources of specialist help

From time to time every teacher of reading feels that she needs help, advice or guidance either with an individual pupil or with a specific problem. The paragraphs which follow attempt to identify some possible sources of assistance for the classroom teacher.

TABLE 12 Types of miscue and possible causes and suggestions for intervention

Type of miscue	Possible Cause
Refusal (silence)	Cannot decode. Lacks confidence to predict. Outside child's experience.
Substitution 1 (wrong word, same meaning)	Reading very fluently (eyes ahead of voice, re-processed text). Good comprehension. Poor text style.
Substitution 2 (wrong word, wrong meaning)	Poor text style. Low comprehension, poor decoding.
Insertion (reads words not there) Omission (leaves out word)	Reading very fluently (eyes ahead of voice, re-processed text.) Poor text style.
Pause Self-correction Repetition	Assessing confusing style of syntax. Assessing ambiguity in the meaning. Misleading text layout.
Intonation rises or falls inappropriately	Misleading text layout. Low comprehension.

	Question	Intervention
1	Is the text too difficult generally (ie miscue rate is higher than one word in 20)?	Suggest less difficult text.
2	Is the word a special noun like the name of someone or somewhere?	Tell the child the word.
3	Is the word outside the child's experience?	Ask the child what he thinks the word should be – what fits the meaning. If he offers a substitution, accept it and tell him the word refused is _____ and that it means the same as substitution 1.
4	Is the word difficult to decode but within the child's experience?	• Tell him to read to end of sentence/ end of line/to next full stop, whichever suits text or child's understanding. Then go back to beginning of sentence and try to fit word in context. or Tell him to start sentence again – get it 'on the run'.

- Ask child what he thinks word should be – what could fit the sense. Then as for 3 above.

- Draw attention to initial consonant and link with sense.

- Draw attention to syllables and known words within the word (eg catapult) and link with initial consonant, sense.

- If all else fails, tell him the word.

Within the school

Very often, a scale post is allocated for reading in particular, or perhaps for language development throughout the school. The person with this responsibility is the obvious choice of colleague to approach if a particular child is having more than average problems with reading. She may have ready-prepared strategies drawn up for recurrent problems encountered by children learning to read. These could be particularly useful if they relate directly to the materials and resources the school has at its disposal.

At Local Authority level

Each education authority usually employs full-time staff who form a Reading Advisory Service. They are specially trained to help individual cases from all the schools within the authority. The way they provide their service differs from authority to authority but usually they work peripatetically, with individuals or groups identified by the class teacher. In some areas, a 'Reading Centre' can be found, where children are taken from their schools, by mini-bus for a number of hours a week. Certain problems identified through learning to read may require specialist medical or psychological help, and if such a case arises teachers should always consult their own headteachers.

National assistance

The Centre for the Teaching of Reading (University of Reading, School of Education, 29 Eastern Avenue, Reading, RG1 5RU, tel Reading 62662/3) is an invaluable source of high quality information. Any queries regarding the teaching of reading may be addressed to the above Centre, which produces leaflets giving sound practical advice for teachers, parents and other helpers on any aspect of teaching reading.

Reading tests

There is a wide selection of reading tests available (see below), but teachers should always be clear about the purposes of each and should test only when there is a specific reason and using an appropriate test. Some possible reasons for testing might include:

- To find a starting point for instruction.
- To compare reading standards in the class with national norms.
- To compare reading standards of pupils within the class.
- To measure reading progress.
- To assess the effectiveness of various approaches to the teaching of reading.
- To diagnose the reading difficulties of individuals (the best possible use of a test – if the results show that a child has scored less than he ought to for his chronological age level, check exactly what his difficulties are, and devise strategies to help him overcome them. Use the tests constructively – they are not meant to be done and then filed away!

The *worst* possible use of a test is to define a curriculum, since only those things which occur in tests will be included.

The teacher needs to decide which of the following type of test matches her reason for testing; eg if she wishes to assess the effectiveness of her method of teaching reading, she may choose to administer a criterion referenced test.

1 *Standardised* eg: Thackeray – Reading Readiness Profile; Schonell – Word Recognition Test; Neale – Analysis of Reading Ability; Carver – Word Recognition Test, Richmond Tests. Different education authorities also often have their own eg The 'Salford Sentence' Reading Test which is given to seven- and eight-year-olds at the end of the summer term.

2 *Criterion-referenced* – divides reading into skills, eg of phonics, such as blends – see page 50.

3 *Informal* – tests made up by the teacher to assess progress in work recently covered.

Unit 7

BUILDING EARLY NUMBER SKILLS

'Mathematics is a way of thinking, ie a discovery of relationships, and the expression of the relationship in symbolic (or abstract) form.' (Mimeo)

Historically, maths has been the bête noire of school children, and held in low esteem by adults!

'That arithmetic is the basest of all mental activities is proved by the fact that it is the only one that can be accomplished by a machine.' (Arthur Schopenhauer)

Negative attitudes militate against effective learning. How, then, can the teacher foster a healthy attitude to maths from the beginning? Below are some basic strategies you might like to try.

- Ensure that number activities in the classroom are seen as worthwhile by pupils.
- Make all number activities immediately relevant to the children's experience.
- Make number activities immediately relevant to what the children are wanting to know.
- Allow pupils regularly to experience a sense of achievement in number work.
- Provide frequent opportunities for pupils to be stretched and challenged through inquiry and problem solving.

Task 27 Fostering positive attitudes to mathematics

Look at the list of strategies above. Devise two or three strategies of your own. If you have the opportunity, try these out. How effective did they prove to be? How would you adapt your approach next time?

In providing number activities for very young children the teacher needs to be aware of the scope and limitations of the infant child's level of thinking, because 'although there is a development which enables children to begin to give reasons for their beliefs and actions, their thinking is still not operational' (Beard 1969). Consequently, relevant activities must be provided which require thinking at the intuitive level or success will not be attained.

It should also be remembered that, while 'small children need to know about maths . . . they also need to discover that learning can be fun' (Potworowska 1985). Every excursion into classroom number work should, as far as possible, be an adventure. If we take the message of Piaget seriously then most maths *evolves* rather than is *imposed*. For example, let us imagine that the class has been on an outing to the coast. How can that experience lead to number education?

The teacher might, on the day, exploit the senses by getting the children to

- count the number of breakwaters they can *see* on the beach;
- count how many different sounds they can *hear* within a set time limit, eg seagull cries, waves on shore, voices etc;
- count how many different textures they can *feel* in collecting shells, seaweed etc.

She could also ask one child to count the children who would like ice cream cones and another to count those who would like ice lollies! Then distribute them – 'Give the children one each' (one to one correspondence).

She might subsequently get the children to

- sort the seaside collections into sets eg shells, pebbles etc;
- make number sets – 'a set of four shells' etc;
- make items for a 'seaside shop' in art and craft for 'sale' in the shop – eg flags and postcards. Collect other items from the classroom – sand toys and buckets and spades from the sand tray, and add items collected on the beach, pebbles, shells etc.

 ## Task 28 Using experiences mathematically

I   Think about one everyday occurrence in the classroom (trips to the coast don't happen every week!). Decide how you might exploit the activity mathematically.

For example: *milk time* –
- conduct a survey of 'Our Favourite Drinks'.
- make a pictogram of the results.
- get the children to interpret the pictorial representation of the results and enrich their number language – 'how many *more* . . . ?'
  'how many *less* . . . ?'
  'how many *equally* popular . . . ?'

2   Note down your chosen activity. Devise some follow-up work which leads from the children's experience to a particular mathematical concept, such as quantity, time or weight.

The assumption made in carrying out Task 28 is that children retain mathematical concepts through considerable amounts of *practical* work and the concepts are reinforced through practice. Thus, Plowden stated as long ago as 1967: 'Children learn mathematical concepts more slowly than we realised. They learn by their own activities . . . Practice is necessary to fix a concept once it has been understood, therefore practice should follow, and not precede, discovery.'

Reviewing published number schemes

The widespread acceptance of the view expressed by Plowden led to the development of number schemes which incorporated the idea of practical work followed by practice to fix the concepts, for example the Nuffield Teachers' Guides. (See the list of selected maths schemes, at the end of this section).

Early criticisms that they did not account for individual interests and strengths were compensated for to an extent by teachers who felt they could 'do their own thing', within what was basically a sound framework.

Thus many teachers devise their own schemes of work to run in conjunction with a published scheme, thus ensuring continuity and steady progression while retaining some teacher autonomy. To pursue such a policy a teacher must know how to assess the value of published schemes, and how to plan a curriculum around them. Table 13 makes some suggestions about ways to evaluate to evaluate a commercial scheme.

Task 29 Evaluating a commercial number scheme

1   Obtain a published maths scheme such as Harold Fletcher's *Maths for Schools*, or the one in use in your school, or one of your own choice. Review the scheme with a view to incorporating it into your own personal scheme and practice.

TABLE 13 Evaluating commercial number schemes: some criteria for judgement

- Does the scheme have a clear rationale, set out in a Teachers' Manual?
- Is the scheme visually attractive so that pupils will want to use it?
- Is the scheme published in a format or variety of formats (eg book, card, equipment-based) which are suitable for your classroom?
- Is the scheme couched in language the pupils will understand?
- How costly is the scheme?
- What is the curriculum content of the scheme:

    - is it suitable?
    - is it in logical sequence?
    - is it practical?
    - does it relate to children's experience?
    - does it offend modern views of eg sexism, racism etc?
    - how does it relate to other schemes in use in the school?

- Does the scheme allow pupils to learn independently of the teacher for reasonable periods of time?
- What learning and teaching methods are implicit in the scheme?
- What life-span would you expect the scheme to have?

2   Work through the scheme, using the criteria set out in Table 13 above.
3   If possible, compare two or three more schemes using the same criteria and procedures.

Task 30 Identifying criteria for effective number schemes

In the light of your findings in Task 29, try to isolate the features of an effective maths scheme for infants. Set these out as a list of criteria.

Devising and implementing a personal scheme of work

In devising a personal scheme of work in mathematics the teacher has to take account of school maths policies; any commercial scheme(s) in use in the school; the criteria of a 'good' scheme as derived from Tasks 29 and 30 above; and opportunities which might arise for 'incidental' learning. It is worth pausing to look at the kinds of incidental learning which are characteristic of infant classrooms.

Thus, on a rainy day, the teacher might ask:

- 'Who wore a pair of wellingtons to school this morning?'
- 'How many do we need to make a pair?'
- 'Did anyone wear a pair of gloves or mittens?'
- 'Put up your hand if you have a pair of hands . . . ears . . . eyes . , . noses?!'

This could lead to some kind of pictorial representation, for instance a pictogram showing number of children who wore wellingtons and number of children who wore shoes.

As we have seen, the teacher needs to start with the children, and in terms of mathematics, they have already begun learning even before starting school. From the minute a child is born he is 'surrounded by space, and he quickly learns to explore, manipulate and control the spatial elements of shape, size and position when attempting to organise his environment' (Choat 1979).

The young child makes deductions for himself, he categorises, classifies and sorts out objects. For example, he discovers that a ball will roll, that blocks need to be built up solidly. But then the child reaches a stage where encouragement and guidance can promote further development. The teacher needs to underpin this secure basis for learning by providing the right kind of experiences and activities in a horizontal development pattern; for as Choat has suggested, 'the child moves backwards and forwards to lower order concepts he has acquired to help him with a new problem' before he progresses. He suggests that the infants' teacher should help the children 'discover how to look' for maths in everyday situations. Table 14 exemplifies this viewpoint.

In developing a personal scheme, then, the teacher needs to work in the knowledge that the child's mathematical development is not linear, and is only partially ordered in terms of higher and lower order concepts. She needs to ensure steady progress, and enrich the activities provided by published schemes while using any spontaneous learning which may occur. A typical outline scheme of number work for four- to seven-year-olds follows in Table 15. Look at the scheme and proceed to Task 31.

Now you have looked over the scheme in Table 15, re-read sections 8 and 9 in the outline scheme. These are vital stages in the child's developing concept of number. The fact that a child can count does not mean that he has understood the *numberness of number* – eg the 'fiveness of five'. Understanding is reached only when the child realises that whatever the arrangement of elements in a set, the numerical value remains the same, and that in counting separate elements, the last number name is the total.

The following activities are suggestions for the promotion of understanding of the numberness of number.

- Make a 'Zoo of Five' for the classroom. A zoo with only five types of animal, or with five of each type.

TABLE 14 Where to find maths

1 *Play:* Outdoor Indoor (Constructional)	• physical activities • games and music, jingles • rhymes, stories, books • manipulative activities (jigsaws, beads, pebbles, toys, structural apparatus)
2 *Semi-structured play*	• home corner • cooking • class shop • sand/water play
3 *Art & craft*	• models • collage • paper cutting • paper folding • plasticine • clay • dough • painting
4 *Nature*	• animals (school pets, pets at home) • growth • time
5 *Buildings*	• the home • the school • the street

- Get the children to talk about numbers. Ask them which is their favourite.
- Make up stories using the numbers.
- Read stories in which numbers play a significant role, eg 'The Three Little Pigs'.
- Sing number rhymes.
- Describe each child in terms of his own numbers: eg 'John is four. He lives at number seven. He has two brothers and one sister. His birthday is on 17 September . . . ' (Height and weight can be added later, as other mathematical topics are covered) (Yardley 1979).

TABLE 15 A number curriculum for the infant school
A scheme of pre-number work

1   Sorting
- General
- Colour
- Shape ⟶ colours and shapes should be taught first
- Attributes of two
- Attributes of three

Number rhymes are a continuous process not a stage.

2   Partitioning

- Colour
- Shape
- General two subsets such as flying/sailing, yellow/not yellow
- Three subsets

3   Matching
Simple practical type

4   Sequencing

5   Comparison
Must stress 'the same as' in addition to 'more than', 'less than'.

6   Ordering

7a   One-to-one (as equivalence)
Must stress, 'Are these enough?' and making sets equal.

7b   One-to-one (as equality)
Give two unequal sets and child matches members and then makes sets equal.

8   Oral counting
Start by counting members of a given set.
Numbers one to five only.

9   *Number symbols*
Numbers one to five only.

10   *Sequencing with numbers*
Numbers one to five only.

11   *Number groups*
Understanding number concepts i.e. the fiveness of five: see p.61
Numbers one to five only.
Go back to stage 8 and repeat up to stage 11 for numbers 6–10.

12   *Number line*
Only to ten, very simple. | 1 | 2 | 3 | 4 | 5 | 6 | 7 | 8 | 9 | 10 |

13   *Numbers as words*
Numbers one to ten.

General Points on 1–13

- This Scheme so far can be covered without the child recording his/her work in writing. This should *not* occur, however, except in the case (very rare) of a child whose motor ability does not reach the same level as his mathematical ability.

- The work must always be done practically before recording is begun.

14   Addition to ten (using apparatus) eg Unifix cubes.
Addition to ten (without use of apparatus).

15   Subtraction to ten (using apparatus).
Subtraction to ten (without use of apparatus).

16   Horizontal addition.
Vertical addition.

17   Number recognition to 20.

18   Addition to 20.

19   Subtraction to 20.

20   Number recognition to 100.

21   Addition of three numbers, horizontally and vertically up to ten.

22   Tens and Units.
Simple addition.

23   Simple subtraction of tens and units.

24   Simple multiplication ('lots of').

25   Simple division ('sharing').

26   Addition of tens and units – 'carrying'.

27   Decomposition.

28   Addition of hundreds, tens and units.

29   Subtraction of tens and units.

30   Times tables – 2, 5, 10, 3, 11, 4, 6, 12.

Topics

Shape

1   Recognition of 2D shapes – circle, square, triangle, rectangle, hexagon, pentagon.

2   Recognition of solid shapes – cube, cuboid, triangular prism, cone, pyramid.

Capacity

1   Water play.

2   Sand play.

3   Language – full, empty, half full, holds more, holds less.

4   Litres.

Weighing

1   Balancing.

2   Language – light, heavy, lighter than, heavier than, weighs more than, weighs less than.

3   Weighing with objects – shells, plasticine, beads, cones.

4   Weighing with standard weights – 10g, 20g, 50g, 100g, 500g, kilo.

Measuring

1   Pre-measurement language:-

larger than, smaller than
heavier than, lighter than
higher than, lower than
longer than, shorter than
holds more than, holds less than
taller than, shorter than
more than, less than
wider than, narrower than

thicker than, thinner than
deeper than, shallower than

2   Improvised units of measurement – body units – hand spans, strides, feet etc.

3   Transitional units of measurement – rods, string, boxes, books etc.

4   Standard units – metre, centimetre.

Time

I   Language – today, tomorrow, before, after, early, late, earlier, later, yesterday, day, month, year, season.

2   Hours.

3   Half hours.

4   Quarter hours.

5   Minutes.

6   Seconds.

Money

I   Coin recognition – I p, 2p, 5p, 10p, 20p, 50p, £1.

2   Addition of coins of same value.

3   Addition of coins of different value.

4   Subtraction of coins.

5   Shopping – simple exchange, all items cost 5p – a coin for an item, mixed prices. Use of lists, giving change, giving bills.

Task 31 Devising number activities

Devise some of your own 'numberness of number' activities. NB. It is useful to have them in the form of classroom displays or as things children can do in spare moments, thus providing the practice and reinforcement referred to earlier.

We have seen that mathematical topics covered in the infant school should be fun for the child and easily related to him and his world – for example, in measurement, use of hand spans, feet etc.

Table 16 further illustrates this theme through an outline of topics to be covered by four- to seven-year-olds in conjunction with the scheme outlined in Table 15.

TABLE 16 Early number work topics to be taught in conjunction with the scheme outlined

Measurement

Simplified model of a measurement concept
Direct comparison
↓
Improvised units, eg body units, hands, feet, etc. It is important to discuss the
limitations of units.
↓
'Transitional' units, eg agreed rods, string, etc.
↓
Standard units, generally speaking unit then sub-unit, eg metre then later
centimetre
↓
Practice and Extension ● a great deal of measuring
● relate to number work

Before this vitally important –
Pre-Measurement Language (see Record Sheet).

Balancing and weighing

Concept of light and heavy: simple work cards. *Balancing* different objects, eg

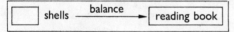

Arbitrary weights eg shells, plasticine etc. Standard weights.

Solid shapes
Recognition and understanding of construction.

Time
Concept of time – before/after
early/late
yesterday/today/tomorrow
Hours, half-hours, quarter-hours, minutes, seconds.
Introduce o'clock – Nursery rhyme, Hickory Dickory Dock.

Money
Coin recognition
Sorting – bronze/silver
Game – *Bus Conductor Game*
Each fare stage is 2p.
Class shop – 1 basic exchange – coin for goods.
2 everything same price, the '10p store'.
3 differing prices and change giving from 5p, 10p, 20p etc.

Capacity
Water play, sand play.
Simple workcards to follow

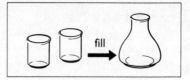

Pictorial representation
Very important, as it is the transitional stage between the practical activity and the symbolisation of numbers and quantities. It translates concrete objects into diagrammatic forms, eg

boys	blue eyes	blue-eyed boys

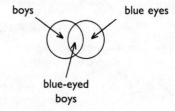

boys   blue eyes

blue-eyed
boys

Mapping

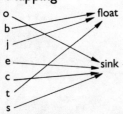

o
b
j   float
e
c   sink
t
s

Matrix eg size of objects

			bowls
			chairs
			beds
			bears
big	middle-sized	small	

Assessing pupil progress in mathematics

The busy infant teacher needs to keep track of each child's progress in order to provide subsequent appropriate learning experiences. Reinforcement could be necessary to prevent another stage being reached prematurely. Each child's response to an activity will be different. It is necessary to keep a simple record of the individual pupil's level of understanding or of any problems found with particular aspects of the number scheme.

Table 17 shows a simple record sheet which requires the teacher to put symbols in the appropriate boxes.

TABLE 17 Number record

Sorting in sets

Odds and ends ....   ☐   √ = child proficient

Shape ....   ☐   / = child needs additional

Colour ....   ☐   practice

Size ....   ☐   X = child needs to re-learn/

Thickness ....   ☐   material not covered

Sub-sets ....   ☐

☐

One-to-one correspondence ....   ☐

Sorting into number sets ....   ☐

Count to five ....   ☐

Count to ten ....   ☐

Number recognition and composition ....   ☐   1–5
6–10

Ordering to ten ....   ☐

Addition to ten

with aids ....   ☐

without aids ....   ☐

Subtraction to ten

with aids ....   ☐

without aids ....   ☐

Addition – horizontally	
– vertically	
Recognition of nos to 20	
Addition to 20	
Subtraction to 20	
Grouping of nos 10–19	
Counting on to 100	
Recognition of nos to 100	
Filling in missing nos	
Addition and subtraction with 3 nos	
Beginning Tens and Units	
Simple addition Tens and Units	
Simple subtraction Tens and Units	
Simple multiplication	
Simple division	
Carrying 1 addition Tens and Units	
Decomposition	
Add Hundreds, Tens and Units	
Subtract Hundreds, Tens and Units	

Tables	2 ×	
	5 ×	
	10 ×	
	3 ×	
	11 ×	
	4 ×	
	6 ×	
	12 ×	

Practical number

Pre-measurement language

Larger than	
Heavier than	
Higher than	
Longer than	

Holds more than	
Taller than	
More than	
Less than	

Long/short
Big/little
High/low
Tall/short
Wide/narrow
Thick/thin

Length/width/height
Full/empty
Deep/shallow
Holds more/less than
Top/bottom
Heavy/light
Balance

Shape

Square	Circle	Rectangle	Triangle	Sphere

Cone	Cylinder	Cuboid	Hexagon	Cube

Measuring

Arbitrary measure

Hand span	Feet	Books	Sticks

Standard measurement

Metre [ ]   cm [ ]   km [ ]

Capacity

Water play [ ]   Sand play [ ]   Problem solving [ ]

Full [ ]   Empty [ ]   Half full [ ]

Litres [ ]   Half-litres [ ]

Money

Coin recognition   1p [ ]   2p [ ]   5p [ ]

10p [ ]   50p [ ]   £1 [ ]

Sub-divide coins [ ]

Addition and subtraction [ ]

Shopping – buying [ ]   selling [ ]

Giving change [ ]   Sharing [ ]   Bills [ ]

Balancing & Weighing

Concept of light and heavy [ ]

Balancing different objects [ ]

Arbitrary weights – shells, plasticine etc [ ]

Standard weights   10g [ ]   20g [ ]   50g [ ]

100g [ ]   500g [ ]   kilo [ ]

Parcels to weigh [ ]

Time
Concept of time – before/after, early/late, yesterday/today/tomorrow

Hours [ ]   Half-hours [ ]   Quarter-hours [ ]

Minutes [ ]   Seconds [ ]

Problem solving [ ]   Use of clock [ ]

It is sometimes appropriate, perhaps for a particular topic, to keep more detailed and sophisticated records than those shown in Table 17. Certainly, detailed records are useful when discussing pupil progress with parents or when trying to help a child with special learning needs. As a postscript to this section you might like to try to devise a way of studying in more detail the work of a single pupil.

Task 32 Tracking number progress

1   Identify one pupil in your class who has special learning needs in mathematics eg a pupil who has been absent for a long time, a slow learner, an especially able pupil, etc.
2   Devise a record-keeping proforma that will
   • track work covered
   • indicate particular deficiencies of understanding
   • seek patterns in the pupil's difficulties (eg poor number formation when writing, low reading ability, colour blindness)
   • help you devise strategies for coping
   • keep able pupils forging ahead.

3   Use the proforma and refine it in use.
4   Use the knowledge you gain to help the pupil to progress. (If necessary, seek specialist help with the evidence of your findings).

Finally in this section on number work we have listed some useful materials, equipment and mathematics schemes for the infant teacher.

Materials for Sorting and Counting

Conkers

Cones

Acorns

Stones

Shells

Peas

Beans

Bottle tops

Marbles

Plastic toys

Beads wooden/plastic

Shapes

Cotton reels

Buttons

Rods

Ribbons/Strings

Counters

Pictures

Sorting trays

Number trays

Number line

Number squares

Equipment

Abacus

Unifix cubes

Unifix pattern boards and trays

Trundle wheel

Metre sticks

Centimetre rulers

Tape measures

Balance for weighing

Improvised metric weights

Materials for weighing

String

Containers with metric capacity

Wooden/plastic cubes

All solid shapes (wooden/plastic)

All plane shapes (wooden/plastic)

Clock face

Egg timer

Brass fasteners

Drinking straws

(Selected) list of mathematics schemes

Mathematics for Schools, Level 1 +
Harold Fletcher, Addison-Wesley (West End House, 11 Hills Place, London
W1).

Outset: Mathematics Card Scheme. Gloucester Maths. workcards, Macmillan
(Houndsmill Estate, Basingstoke, Hampshire).

Groundwork: Mathematics
J.Lowe and M.Sutton, Macmillan.

Bulmershe: Materials and Handbooks. ESA (Pinnacles) P O Box 22, Harlow,
Essex.

Roots of Number Dr Ernest Choat, Cassell (35 Red Lion Square, London WC1).

Science 5–13 published by Macdonald Educational (Holywell House, Worship
Street, London EC2) for the Schools' Council.

Unifix: Activity cards. Philograph Publications (marketed by Philip and Tacey,
North Way, Andover, Hampshire).

I Can Count Wheaton (Hernock Road, Exeter).

Number Time M.Maughan, S.E.Maughan and G.P.Winder, Univ. of London
Press (Hodder & Stoughton Educational, PO Box 6, Mill Road, Dunton Green,
Sevenoaks, Kent).

Multilink Materials and handbook ESA.

Let's Think About Maths, Leonard Sealey, Nelson (Lincoln Way, Windmill
Road, Sunbury on Thames).

Kites leading to *Maths Adventure* by Jan Standfield, Evans.

Nuffield Maths One and Two Longman.

Mathematics Heinemann *Infant* Scottish Education Dept.

Mathematics – The First Three Years Chambers.

Early Mathematical Experiences (Addison Wesley).

Childsplay Mathematics J.Stephens et al, Evans.

For further reading

Nuffield Maths. Project publications 1–6
I Do and I Understand : Pictorial representation : Beginnings: Maths begins:
Shape and Size : Computation and Structure. John Murray.

'Foundations of Maths in the Infant School' Joy Taylor. George Allen & Unwin

'Children's Acquisition of Mathematics' NFER, Dr Ernest Choat.

Unit 8

ENCOURAGING LANGUAGE SKILLS

Conscious and incidental language learning, speaking and listening

'All children talk and make sense from what they hear others say' (Rosen 1973). Through talking, children learn, and they do this 'in a very complex way'. It has been suggested that three processes are involved: 'firstly, a child must have experience of language, secondly, he must have experience of the world, thirdly he must be able to organise his thinking so that he makes sense of both kinds of experience.' (Rosen *op cit*)

The teacher needs to consider what kind of talk the child needs to experience, and in what conditions he or she needs to hear it. This latter point we have looked at in some detail in other sections, eg in examining the need to create a 'literacy' environment with stimulating displays, especially the use of books themselves in displays (Unit 17).

In addressing the first point, the teacher needs to capitalise on naturally occurring talk in the classroom as well as more structured interchanges. Here are some examples.

- Before registration, the children often rush into the classroom, bursting with enthusiasm, and are keen to tell the teacher and the class something of interest to them which has happened over the weekend or during the last evening. This spontaneity should not be discouraged, but rather encouraged. If the children are made to wait until after assembly perhaps their enthusiasm will have waned.
- At 'story-time', allow one of the children to tell a short story.

- Set up an 'interview' between two children or one child and yourself. The children can answer as 'themselves', or as famous personalities, about their birthday party or a television programme they have just appeared in. If a project on which the class has been working involved a central character, this could be another 'interviewee'.
- Children could be asked to give a report, like a television newsreader on items of recent world news. Children are often very well-informed of events happening locally and on a world scale.
- Play games, for example 'The Safari Game' (essentially a descriptive exercise but which encourages the 'enquire-and-eliminate' procedure). One child thinks of an animal and describes it feature by feature. The other children take turns to guess the name of the animal after each feature. The child who guesses correctly can then think of their own animal to describe. This game could be played with a number of different subjects.
- Ask the children to give directions or instructions, eg how something in the classroom works.

Rich experience is not enough; the extension of language skills is essential and the teacher needs to help the child extend his skills in recall, projection, reasoning and imagination (compare Tough 1977).

She can do this by:

- introducing a theme and developing new ways of exploring it.
- setting an example of how to discuss things.
- not allowing the more verbose individuals to obscure what the other children are trying to say.
- being a good listener herself, allowing the child to finish what he is saying.
- elaborating on the child's explanations, helping him to express his thoughts.
- opening up new possibilities in his talk, or alternatively, following up one single idea, concentrating on one experience and working it through.
- helping them use their language and think in different ways – 'What makes you think that?'; 'Why did you say that?'; 'What would happen if . . . ?'
- asking them to discuss and compare things which will help them to make logical choices between alternatives.

Task 33 Developing use of language

In the preceding paragraphs we have considered four areas of language development which a teacher can promote:
- Recall
- Projection

- Reasoning
- Imagination

Take each of the four areas in turn and devise a simple strategy of your own for use in your classroom.

Try each strategy out and refine it as neceessary.

Reading

The conscious and systematic development of reading skills by the teacher is discussed in Unit 6. But what about the 'unconscious' learning that takes place in the classroom with regard to reading?

> 'Visually there is nothing in reading that the eye and brain doesn't already do when a child looks around a room to locate a specific toy or a piece of furniture.' (Smith 1971)

The many captions, instructions, labels, information and lists to be found in the majority of infant classrooms rely for their effectiveness on such visual acuity and the child's natural curiosity. The function of the brain is to connect up the many clues which lead to the children recognising the words or sentence, whatever method they use – look and say, phonic etc.

This is one form of 'incidental' language learning. The child is discovering for himself that language has many uses; that we need language to communicate, to gain information and to organise ourselves in work and play. Labels stating 'All our class went to the zoo', 'This is a picture of the astronaut leaving the lunar module to collect some samples of rock', 'Here is our milk rota', 'Four children are allowed in the Home Corner', would illustrate such uses.

It has been noted (Clay 1972) that during the first two years of learning to read, the child learns, either consciously or unconsciously,

- attention to aspects of print;
- some relations between print and oral language;
- the kinds of strategies that maintain fluency;
- the kinds of strategies that explore detail;
- the kinds of strategies that increase understanding;
- the kinds of strategies that detect and correct errors.

First steps in written language: from speaking to writing

When a child starts school, he is used to communicating by speaking. It is a totally natural means of communication, whereas writing is not, and has to be learnt. The child had to *learn* to speak, but writing is a more abstract activity. The teacher needs to help his understanding of written language by:

- showing him the connections between his thoughts, the words he speaks, and marks on paper.
- showing him (as his skills develop), how to listen to his 'inner voice', his own thoughts, and write them on paper, without speaking them out loud.
- showing him the uses of writing and its value, its superiority to talking; its lasting qualities; the fact that it allows us time to think carefully before we communicate our thoughts; the way we can give much more detail to our work in the written form.
- ensuring that the child sees the teacher writing, for different purposes, and enjoying it.

Secretarial skills: pre-writing

There has been a great deal of criticism in recent years of pre-writing patterns, mainly on the grounds that they can quite often be more difficult to produce than actual letters. More emphasis has been placed on the need to encourage 'scribble patterns' instead, which resemble letter shapes. It is believed that children put more effort into their drawings and prepare themselves better for writing through their drawings than through practising writing patterns. Their use has been changed by many to the encouragement of faster writing with a flow, once the child knows how to form letters.

There is much controversy concerning the stage at which a child is 'ready to write' but many teachers believe that the child's drawings are a good indication of such readiness (Michael 1984). If the child can draw a person with correctly placed details and shows the ability to draw one shape inside another, then on this theory he is ready to write: see Table 18.

Once identified as 'ready to write' the child can go on to learn the secretarial skills of letter formation.

Early attempts at writing

The traditional method of teaching writing, in the very early stages, has been for the teacher to ask the child to illustrate any news he may have and then ask him to tell her about it. She then writes down his comments (he sees that his thoughts can be written down as marks on paper). The child may then trace over the top of the words and later 'underwrite' the words. Later still, he will provide his own captions.

The method is fundamentally a sound one, but care must be taken to ensure that mindless 'labelling' does not result: 'Here is a dog', 'Here is my house'.

TABLE 18 Judging writing readiness

Ready to write

Almost ready

Not yet ready

Since this form of 'writing' can continue for weeks, even months, the child needs to be encouraged to give an opinion, or express a feeling about the picture eg 'I like eating spaghetti. It makes my face sticky and orange', instead of 'I am eating my tea'.

Developing early writing skills

The teacher should always encourage the child to write freely about things which interest him, but she also needs to structure the development in writing skills with specific strategies (SCHOLA 1982).

Some examples of possible exercises the teacher can devise are:

- wordless pictures – the children supply the story;
- cartoon strips minus the words – the children have to fill in the words in the balloons;
- words which evoke emotions – 'sadness is . . .', 'happiness is . . .' The children complete the sentence and compose a story, perhaps from their own experience, which illustrates that emotion;
- questions to be answered, eg 'How do you bake a cake?' The children need to provide detailed instructions for a number of activities;

- a contribution to a book, eg 'Ouch' book, in which each page must be completed by an individual child as in 'I was stung by a nettle – ouch!'

The teacher can also encourage development by helping children with:

- the invention of characters – by reading well-chosen stories;
- the creation of different settings – by asking – 'Where did your character live? What else was near the place? Was it day-time or night time? What was the time exactly? What was the weather like?' etc;
- the use of many first hand experiences;
- the use of past experiences – in constructional play, domestic play, imaginative play and creative play as well as the child's experiences at home;
- the development of a story with a beginning, a middle and an end – first steps towards a real 'structure' in his stories. (By the end of the infant school this stage can hopefully be reached).

The teacher must be aware of the need to give the child as much opportunity as possible for creative, expressive writing and must avoid concentrating all her efforts on providing workcards and cards to copy to develop particular skills. A balance needs to be achieved in order that the child enjoys writing and finds it rewarding (Lane 1984).

Expanding vocabulary

Some of the strategies we have already discussed for developing language skills have included examples which would help in expanding vocabulary, but it is worth stressing this as a process in its own right.

Many children have a great many more words at their disposal than they ever use in common speech, or in their writing at school. The teacher needs to encourage them to enjoy using words effectively and to 'collect' words which sound exciting. Games can be played, eg 'I went shopping'; 'I went shopping and I bought a pound of apples' (first child); 'I went shopping and I bought a pound of apples and a bag of jumping beans' (second child) etc. A variation on this theme is 'The pirate had a face' (first child); 'The pirate had a frightening face' (second child); 'The pirate had a scarred, frightening face' (third child).

 ## Task 34 Extending pupils' vocabulary

Make a list of six different strategies (excluding playing games of the kind described in the text) which you can use in your own classroom to promote the extension of pupils' vocabulary. Include here any strategies that make children 'word conscious'.

Unit 9

SOCIAL AND MORAL LEARNING

The purpose of this aspect of curriculum is to help the child to make moral choices and to become socially aware and responsible. In this role, the teacher is only one of the major influences in the child's development; others would include the child's parents, television, and the peer group. The teacher needs to remember that the practice of parents will vary greatly (Downey and Kelly 1978) in the attention they give to their role. They may adopt an approach which is extremely authoritarian, or a more democratic view, or even one which is laissez-faire. Child-rearing practices vary from the use of a quick slap as a form of punishment, to a reasoned debate and gentle persuasion. Children who are given reasons for certain required actions tend to formulate a rationale for their own behaviour more easily than those who are told 'Because I say so' as a substitute for an explanation.

Television also has a profound influence on the young child and his developing attitudes. Disruptive behaviour on the screen, as in the classroom or playground, suggests that the child/adult/actor gaining most attention is the one displaying the most anti-social tendencies. Very often, lasting impressions are made of these hostile, selfish attitudes.

On the other hand, pro-social behaviour can also be encouraged through the medium of television (or comics). Good is often seen to triumph over evil in cartoon programmes. In the USA, one particular programme's hero, Mr Rogers, acts in an especially pro-social manner, sharing the feelings of other people and making sacrifices for someone else without expecting a reward (Woolfson 1985).

Task 35 Exploring children's heroes or heroines

Ask a random selection of the children in your class to name their favourite three cartoon-type programmes from television. (This should not be a problem. Breakfast television and Saturday morning children's television have an abundance of these – 'He-Man' etc).

Ask them to write or tell you the name of their favourite characters in each one. The results will be interesting in that they will show the popularity of either the 'baddies' or the 'heroes'.

Discuss with the children the reasons for their choices.

The peer group's influence only really comes into the ascendancy in adolescence, but its contribution is worth noting by the teacher – especially by age seven, when 'gangs' often form which have collective values and attitudes.

Defining the teacher's role

The teacher contributes to the child's developing social and moral awareness in two ways (that is, deliberately and unconsciously) through what has been termed the 'hidden curriculum'. It has been said (Downey and Kelly 1978) that 'As much, if not more, is learnt from the way in which they (teachers) organise the work of their pupils, react to the behaviour of individuals, use punishment, exercise discipline, achieve control, and, in general, approach their pupils, handle their classes and manage their classrooms. Moral attitudes are caught from every interaction of teacher and pupil.'

The very length of time a teacher spends with her class in itself means that she will be a major influence in the fostering of positive/negative attitudes, as Woolfson's (1985) research demonstrates. Two matched groups of children spent a great deal of time with an adult. The adult behaved in a very altruistic and empathetic way at times of distress with the first group, but with aloofness at similar times with the second group. Results showed that children in the first group were more likely to act in an altruistic way in situations than were those in the second group.

Having realised the importance of the teacher's role, how can the teacher ensure that she is a competent social and moral educator? McPhail (1982) makes a number of suggestions:

- If you do not like and do not feel sympathy for children and young people, do not teach. You will be doing yourself and the young a favour.
- Preserve a personal 'value balance'. Marshalling your full rational and emotional forces over trivia leaves you with no reserves when the really important issues emerge.

- Keep, or try to keep, a sense of humour.
- Believe in yourself, but never assume you know it all.
- Be prepared to admit your mistakes.
- Be as honest as you can with yourself and others.
- Don't indulge your secret sorrows.
- Avoid passing on 'demarcation' attitudes.
- Establish relevance in all that you do without preaching about it.

Although the teacher must realise the potential of the 'hidden curriculum' as a social and moral educator, she also needs to take *deliberate* steps to plan the child's social and moral development. These could be based upon a scheme which starts from the child himself, his own self-awareness within his own environment, and then moves out.

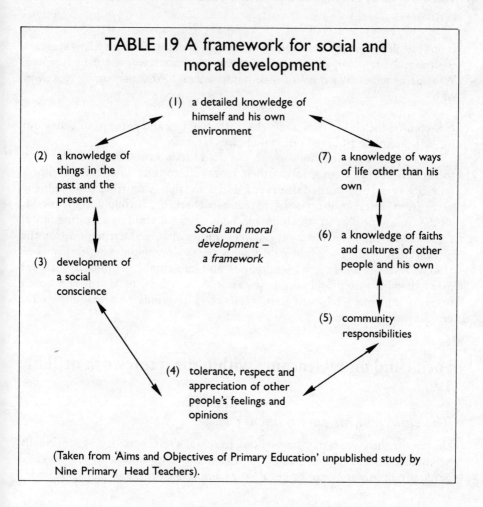

TABLE 19 A framework for social and moral development

(1) a detailed knowledge of himself and his own environment

(2) a knowledge of things in the past and the present

(3) development of a social conscience

Social and moral development – a framework

(7) a knowledge of ways of life other than his own

(6) a knowledge of faiths and cultures of other people and his own

(5) community responsibilities

(4) tolerance, respect and appreciation of other people's feelings and opinions

(Taken from 'Aims and Objectives of Primary Education' unpublished study by Nine Primary Head Teachers).

This plan is obviously an overview and is applicable to the whole primary age range: it extends beyond the infant stage, but it is useful as a framework within which to plan individual strategies. The teacher needs to provide specific content for the developing morality of the child for three reasons.

The first is that children need 'rules, norms, criteria of choice and standards of behaviour' (Downey and Kelly 1978) because they need to make choices – not huge moral dilemmas at the infant level, but choices nevertheless: whether to take something from the teacher's desk when she isn't looking; whether to own up when another child is being blamed for making a mess in the wet area when it was he who splashed water everywhere and threw out all the water toys.

Task 36 Observing social and moral behaviour in the classroom

Spend half an hour in the classroom of a colleague (if possible) or in a fellow student's classroom. Note down all the choices children are faced with and their reactions. What percentage 'owned up' to their misdemeanors? What percentage 'got away with it'?

Secondly, the child needs to develop settled habits and patterns of behaviour for self discipline to make rational choices later on.

Thirdly, Downey and Kelly argue, the child needs a content based on reality to provide the 'raw material' of their moral education. As already outlined, morality cannot be learned or practised in a vacuum. Contributions are being made from different directions – parents, teachers, peer group and the media, all the time. The way in which the teacher assists the child in acquiring moral values must take the form of *guidance* rather than indoctrination, for the obvious reason that the infant child is at his most vulnerable and impressionable. Simply because he is now autonomous and can think for himself does not mean that his moral and social education is complete; he is still very much open to influence. To exert that influence is a serious responsibility and a critical part of the teacher's professionalism.

Social and moral learning within the framework of Table 19

The child and his environment

During the three years of infant school, the child's self awareness is continually heightened as his identity develops within the class and school. The child gradually becomes aware of his abilities and self-worth, and gains some idea of his location in the class, in the school, in the family, and geographically. The teacher can extend this growing awareness and help it mature through work on 'Myself'; 'My family'; 'Things I like doing'; 'Things I don't like doing'; 'What makes me sad'; 'What makes me happy'; 'My friends'; 'My school'; 'My house' (and garden); 'My town'.

Past and present

By the time the child leaves the infant school he or she should have been given the opportunity to explore the local environment carefully, visit places of local significance and discover local social history at museums and buildings of historical interest.

Developing a social conscience

In the infant school, responsibility is often seen as a reward for good behaviour. For example, if a child has been particularly well-behaved, he is often rewarded by the task of looking after the class pets that day. But caring for animals is an excellent way of developing responsibility in those who continually show anti-social tendencies as well as the more pro-social members of the class.

Recent research has suggested that a teacher should spend less time discouraging disruptive behaviour in the classroom and playground in the more usual interventionist ways, and should actively foster a sense of responsibility and a social conscience, illustrating on every possible occasion how altruism and empathy are the best means to an enjoyable school and home life. Of course, a sensible balance has to be maintained between methods of class management and discipline, but all teachers would do well to reflect upon the issues.

Developing tolerance, respect and appreciation of other people's feelings and opinions

Tolerance, or lack of it, is well illustrated in the first year class of any infant school. Many children, despite having brothers and sisters at home, and despite nursery or play-group experience, find sharing very difficult to accept. It is a question of careful management on the part of the teacher to alleviate problems which give rise to cries of 'She won't let me be the mummy . . . ', 'He won't let me play with the helicopter' and 'I'm not playing any more if she does that . . . ' It is very difficult to tolerate the views of another if they happen to lead to a game being taken over or spoilt or changed in any way. Allocating children to different activities is an obvious means by which the teacher can share resources, usually assigning maximum numbers to an activity, eg four in the Home Corner. But these are temporary measures, and more will be necessary to help children control their own sharing behaviour.

Respect for other children as well as adults is an important trait in many different ways. For example, if a game is taking place which needs only two players, or if apparatus available means that only two children may be involved in that particular activity, then a third child must learn to respect the other children's need to continue alone undisturbed. He can take his turn later (Evans 1979). It has been found that if children are shown this consideration, they are more likely to be persuaded to make the same concessions to other children.

In fact, it has been demonstrated that a child can show signs of empathy and altruism very early so it is not so unusual that the child can appreciate the feelings of other people when they are the same as his, or when they are in opposition to his feelings at that time. Simple observation will show that a 48-hour-old baby will cry when he hears others cry, and is obviously able to react to emotional reactions of those around him. By age two, a child has lost some of his self-centredness and will, for example, comfort his mother if she is upset. At age four empathy has increased, but altruism has not quite caught up. Thus it has been noted that a child of four shows concern for an injured person, but may not do anything to help. This is where the teacher can intervene with the notion of caring for and helping people in need. An excellent story to illustrate this is *That's what friends are for* by Florence Parry Heide and Sylvia Worth van Clief (Scholastic Book Services 1968). When Theodore the Elephant breaks his leg and cannot meet his cousin at the edge of the forest, what can he do? His friends give advice which doesn't solve his problem, but then one finally comes along with a practical solution of help!

The child needs to learn to control both behaviour and emotions. This is linked with the need for courtesy and good manners both in and out of school. This need is often demonstrated very well in the infant school when a child clamours to speak to the teacher immediately, whether she is otherwise occupied or not. In the reception class in particular, prodding fingers will attempt to gain the teacher's attention from all angles as several children at once try to gain her attention. Voices usually become raised, and it is then necessary for the teacher to explain that she can only speak to one child at a time, and that others must wait until she or the child she is speaking with have finished.

The same situation arises in class discussions and it must be made clear that each person should be allowed to talk whilst the others listen, and vice versa.

It is also necessary to foster good habits of cleanliness and hygiene, in a personal sense as well as in the classroom. At 'cleaning-up-time' the children need to be responsible in their attitude even if they didn't play with the apparatus in the area which they have been asked to tidy. They should quickly realise that if everyone helps the task is much easier. They also need to take good care of various pieces of apparatus, making sure equipment is put away properly in the appropriate boxes and drawers and not mixed up with other items in the wrong place.

To be positive, too, the teacher needs to point out acts of kindness each time she witnesses them. Children respond to praise so well that these incidents could occur more often. The major consideration is that the children see justice being done in classroom life and attempt to reproduce it in their life outside the classroom, with their friends and family.

Task 37 Watching misbehaviour and how teachers handle it

Observe a lesson in a colleague's classroom. Use a proforma such as the one below to record examples of misbehaviour and how the teacher dealt with them. Afterwards discuss your findings with the colleague to complete columns 3 and 4.

DURING LESSON		AFTER LESSON	
Brief description of misbehaviour	Action taken by teacher (if any)	Reason for teacher's action or non-intervention	Reflections on alternative strategies
1			
2			

Community responsibilities

The child of four, five, six or seven can be seen to cope well with the idea of people acting in groups, not only acting on immediate problems, but on longer term projects. For example, collections were made by thousands of primary school children for the starving in Ethiopia in 1985/6. This shows that not only can this age group show empathy for others in their immediate community, but that of the much wider community in whatever country help is seen to be needed. A sensitive teacher can foster this kind of attitude; and it is an area where the media are particularly useful in highlighting current issues and contemporary problems.

Developing a knowledge of other faiths, cultures and ways of life

This is the point at which some consideration needs to be given to the role of religious education in the infant school. Kerry (1984) has argued that there are three aspects to RE in school:

Religious knowledge

This consists of factual knowledge about one's own and other people's religions. It would include some awareness of stories from the Bible, the Qur'an, the Talmud or other appropriate scriptures. It would demand some familiarity with very basic beliefs (Christians believe Jesus Christ rose from the dead on Easter Day) with symbols (the Cross), with festivals and with religious rituals (baptism, bar-mitzvah) and places of worship (synagogues, mosques, churches).

Moral education

All religions make statements about how people should behave. Similarly, agnostics and atheists generally have some form of moral code. Considerations of right and wrong, and the reasons and arguments that support differing viewpoints, are relevant here.

Spiritual response

Every religion eventually demands of the individual a commitment: 'I believe', 'Do this'.

The stance of this book is clear, but debatable. It is that imparting religious knowledge is a legitimate role of the teacher in a secular school: in today's society this knowledge may according to circumstance be more or less weighted towards Christianity, though since this faith is deeply embedded in our indigenous culture it should not be thrust aside. It is crucial that moral education takes place and that all varieties of reason and opinion are reflected and discussed. In the 1960s and 1970s Stenhouse (1970) argued that in presenting these issues teachers should be wholly neutral; but many honest professionals find this view impossible or unacceptable. There is, however, no place in secular schools for RE which seeks commitment from pupils to a specific creed, and whether RE results in a spiritual response is often something the teacher cannot know.

Another important consideration in the infant school is that of 'readiness' and this has been referred to in other contexts, eg those of reading, number and writing. Ageing but still useful researches by Ronald Goldman (1964, 1965) demonstrated that Piagetian insights could be obtained about the processes by which children learn about religion. Since religious education demands a grasp of quite difficult concepts and of abstract notions much of it cannot adequately be grasped by infants. At this age it is often safer from all points of view to stick to the moral issues and to the concepts that derive from these issues.

At this stage, RE can be concerned with the child's self-awareness, relationships and the world around us (Gregory 1980) and there are many picture books which explore these themes beautifully:

Self-awareness – stories which evoke different emotions encourage the child to imagine how he would feel in certain situations, and to talk about similar experiences he has had. *A baby sister for Frances* by Russell Hoban (Puffin) concerns feelings of jealousy, for example. *There's a nightmare in my cupboard* by Mercer Meyes (Dent) and *The owl who was afraid of the dark* by Jill Tomlinson (Puffin) are both concerned with fear, and will stimulate good discussions.

Relationships – sensitivity to other people's feelings is beautifully written into the story of *Dogger* by Shirley Hughes (Bodley Head), always a firm favourite, and one which gets the same reaction ('wasn't Bella kind . . . ') every time.

The world around us – as the child takes an interest in the environment and nature it is worth focussing on the changing scenes of seasons. *The happy owls* by Celestine Piatti (Benn) and *The tree* by Lela Mari (Dent) illustrate well this approach.

These themes and others like them can be explored well in a school assembly format, together with celebrations of major festivals in the Christian year and in other faiths. Hopefully, school worship will then fulfil the criteria laid down by an ILEA advisory council for RE, that it should 'engage children in an exploration of that which has meaning, value and purpose for them'. (ILEA 1985). With these thoughts in mind you might like to tackle the last activity in this section.

Task 38 Collecting stories useful in social and moral learning

Obtain a set of filing cards and a box in which to store them. Start a card index of stories which might be useful in promoting social and moral learning. Keep the material under suitable sub-headings (eg Caring, Jealousy, Sharing). Add to the index whenever you discover new and appropriate materials. Record title, author, publisher, date and *where the material is located* so that you can find it quickly as the need arises.

Unit 10

THE ENVIRONMENT AS A RESOURCE

The infant age is the age of immediacy, the time to touch, taste, smell, look and listen. The world in which the young child finds himself or herself is exciting and full of wonder, but at times it may be intimidating, puzzling or full of dread. Either way, the teacher has the task of helping the child to explore, understand and come to terms with it.

Environmental education is a broad label and it is helpful to consider some definition of it. Frequently in practice it is interpreted in a way that implies a 'subject' bias. Environmental education for some teachers is the exploration of nature, from the school field to the local canal or farmland: the bias is scientific. For others the emphasis can be labelled historical; and the activities centre around churches, or old mills, or castles. But true environmental education, we suggest, does not recognize these boundaries. It takes the world in which the child lives and explores it in ways that cross traditional boundaries of subject, of time and so on. The child explores with his senses the environment in which he or she lives (my home, my family, my road, my neighbourhood, my school, my village or town, my county, my country) and in the process is guided by need towards using more systematic means by which to classify what is discovered. These means are the embryonic methods of procedure or disciplines of what are discovered later to be 'subjects'. Thus the child who looks at his home and family will develop the need for classifying information in time-scales (my Mum does, my Gran did); and so some measure of 'historicity' is born into his thinking. The need to express to others what has been learned may result in making a bar chart through which mathematical concepts are promoted, and so on.

The great strength of the primary phase of education is its freedom to explore without the *pre-condition* of using traditional methods and disciplines. It is this characteristic which supplies its creativeness and the freshness that comes through in the child's view of his or her circumstances.

So these paragraphs have both expounded a philosophy and hinted at a curriculum. Environmental education begins from the child in his place and time and marches steadily outwards towards the horizons of his perceptions, aiming always to broaden and extend them. Some of this atmosphere is nicely conveyed in the outline syllabus of part of an Environmental Studies scheme by Cast (1978) given in Table 20.

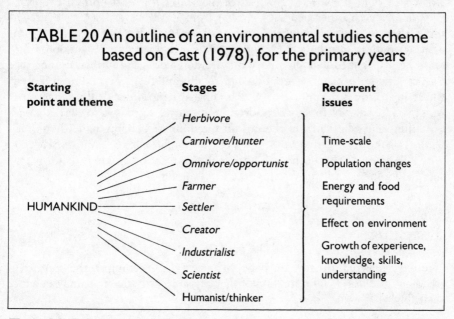

TABLE 20 An outline of an environmental studies scheme based on Cast (1978), for the primary years

Starting point and theme	Stages	Recurrent issues
	Herbivore	
	Carnivore/hunter	Time-scale
	Omnivore/opportunist	Population changes
	Farmer	Energy and food requirements
HUMANKIND	Settler	
	Creator	Effect on environment
	Industrialist	Growth of experience, knowledge, skills, understanding
	Scientist	
	Humanist/thinker	

Task 39 Devising an outline syllabus for environmental education

Devise an outline syllabus for environmental education for the 5–7 age-range. If you work in an urban or suburban school devise one suitable for children from a rural area and vice versa.

When you have completed your outline try to think back to answer these questions:

• Did you find this exercise difficult?
• In what ways?
• Did you find it easy to empathize with children from a contrary environment to that of your own school?
• To what extent did you have to acquire new knowledge yourself in order to complete the task?
• How effectively do you think you could now expand, resource and teach your outline syllabus?

It has been suggested that children learn about the environment through experience, and that such experience is essentially 'first-hand', ie through the senses. The next few paragraphs examine what can be done to sharpen children's sensory awareness in an environmental context.

Seeing

The use of sight is the most obvious of the senses for most normal children. Eye contact with other people is crucial from birth onwards (Argyle 1967), and the removal of eye contact disorientates even adults. But we also rely on sight to organize our daily lives, and to a remarkable degree. If you doubt the centrality of sight to daily living try blindfolding yourself and then finding the correct money to pay the monthly bill to the milkman, or finding a stored object in a crowded cupboard; and boiling an egg is decidedly dangerous! Perhaps a good way to show children how crucial sight is is to play a game like blind man's buff or pin the tail on the donkey. Having made the point, Table 21 suggests positive ways in which you might help children *consciously* to use their eyes. The purpose is to raise *awareness* of looking, to form the *habit* of looking, and to encourage *critical* looking.

Listening

We have referred already, on page 44, to careful listening in the context of reading readiness. Here are some other possible activities that may enhance listening.

- The 'pass the message' game, where each player passes on as accurately as possible a message whispered by the previous player.
- Identifying everyday sounds (from a prepared tape).
- Identifying or trying to guess at less familiar sounds.
- Learning 'sound' words: quiet, noisy, loud, soft, squeak, creak, bang, cheep, sigh etc.
- Inventing sounds: children make their own from apparatus supplied (eg elastic bands, tin lids, beakers, water).
- Discriminating between musical instruments.
- Finding out what can be heard from the playground (school bell, chatter, traffic, factories working, bird sound).
- Listening to the sound of silence.

TABLE 21 Exercises to improve seeing as a skill

- Playing games, such as 'I spy'
- Discriminating colours, shades, shapes
- Spotting similarities and differences
- Seeing in close-up using magnifying glasses, microscopes
- Looking into the distance: using binoculars, telescope
- Looking words: peep, stare, gaze etc
- Drawing from life ie accurate copying
- Looking and recalling games: describing an object seen briefly then hidden
- Using a range of words for things seen, eg big *could* be gigantic, large, enormous
- Spotting comparatives: bigger, smaller, longer, wider, deeper
- Learning about standpoint: views from above, below etc
- Discovering how other creatures see: owls, dragonflies, bats
- Giving messages visually: beacons, flags, hand signals
- Using flashcards
- Identification games (birds, cars, uniforms etc)
- Describing accurately what is seen
- Playing games based on visual cues: eg charades
- Making jig-saw puzzles
- ....
- ....
- .... (add your own ideas here)

- Describing animal noises: grunt, squeal, moo, honk, bray, scratch, hiss etc.
- Trying one's own voice: what sounds can it produce?

You might find it useful to add your own to the list we have provided to get you started.

Tasting and smelling

The sense of taste, linked as it is physiologically with the sense of smell, is an important one in daily life but one not always appreciated in education. Teenage boys in chemistry lessons become fascinated by hydrogen sulphide; but teachers as a whole don't find the taste/smell skills particularly enlightening. Yet in the world of the small child they are; and they are an important factor in environmental education. Flowers smell; so does a diesel engine on a juggernaut. In the same street at 5 am the flowers scent the air while by 8 am everything else may be drowned out by the diesel fumes.

Safety is an important factor here. Teachers must be aware, and must advise children, *not* to sniff indiscriminately or put potentially dangerous things in the mouth or near the nose. Children need their judgements trained but can be safely educated to use scent and taste to explore their worlds. So you might try:

- raising awareness by making safety posters about things *not* to sample (berries, fungi);
- smelling ingredients in common use in cooking, and tasting some products;
- comparing and describing the scents of wild flowers;
- tasting blindfold to identify substances;
- compiling taste and smell words: bitter, sweet, salty; soft, chewy, crunchy etc.

Touching

The young child's instinctive reaction to any object in the environment is to grasp it and explore it through touch. In the passage that follows a short extract from a case-study of a lesson brings together the 'sensory' approach advocated in this and the preceding paragraphs. The children here really are *exploring* their environment.

WHEELS

'... One group began the construction of cardboard carts. They had to cut out circles to make the wheels, but also to work out where the centre was to make the pinholes for the axles or they wouldn't run true. They constructed some mock medieval roads, and found them very bumpy; so then they had to try to find ways of putting a rim on the wheel so it didn't stick so easily in the ruts.

One group worked with a parent, trying to make a wooden wheel from a slice of log, hammering with sharp pieces of wood and stone. After about half an hour these children decided it was hard work! The wood split and they concluded that the early wheel-makers either used different types of wood or they treated it differently. One child suggested soaking the wood over night.

Later we went down to the farmyard in the village, looking at the machinery there, feeling the big treads of the tractor tyres and measuring ourselves next to the wheels of the articulated truck . . . '

To sum up, then: so far in this section we have looked at the nature of environmental studies, some curriculum considerations, and how to equip children with the sensory tools to explore their own environments. Thus the youngsters can more effectively exploit and extend their natural curiosity; a key issue in infant education. Let us now switch the focus of attention to the teacher. What skills does she need in order to be effective in this area? First try Task 40, then consult Table 22.

Task 40 Deciding on qualities required of an environmental studies teacher

In the light of what has been said so far what do you feel are the skills and qualities requisite in an effective teacher of environmental education? Jot down some notes of your own, then ask two or three colleagues to make suggestions. Compile your collection of ideas into a list and compare your collected professional wisdom with that in Table 22.

Topic or thematic work

As we have seen already, environmental education is often tackled thematically or in the form of a topic (Bradley et al 1985). Topic planning is an important skill in its own right. It is not sufficient just to hang work rather casually

---

TABLE 22 Some qualities and skills needed by the effective teacher of environmental education

Qualities	Skills
• Genuine interest in a wide range of subjects from drain-covers to space-probes	• Knowing where to find information
	• Tracking down, storing, retrieving and using resource materials
• Infectious enthusiasm	• Exploiting a varied approach to lesson activity and teaching method
• Keenness to work outdoors	
• Curiosity and an enquiring mind	• Exhibiting a meticulous approach to planning learning experiences and out-of-classroom work
• A broad, general knowledge	
	• Showing a creative approach to devising and setting classroom tasks

Add your own as a result of Task 40.

around a current schools' television series; nor to collect materials around a theme and then use them unsystematically. A preparation checklist for topic work was compiled from questionnaire responses and case studies of teachers at work by a Schools' Council project on topic work (School Curriculum Development Committee 1985), and the advice given there appears as Table 23.

TABLE 23 Preparing for topic work

Before the topic begins, teachers should

1. *Prepare content and teaching methods*
    - Make flow diagrams or outlines of anticipated directions of study
    - Divide the content into the curriculum areas to be covered
    - Decide on specific teaching activities or modes for sub-division of the content
    - Refer to the school's outline scheme of work
    - Read around the subject at their own level
    - Make a list of the skills to be taught
    - Make notes on classroom management procedures (e.g. assign pupils to working groups)
    - Decide on the time-scale of the topic
    - Amend flowcharts or plans in consultation with pupils
    - Plan lead lessons

2. *Prepare resources and materials*
    - Make a search of school and public libraries
    - Collect suitable audiovisual software
    - Arrange visits and speakers
    - Contact museums and other outside organizations
    - Prepare worksheets or assignment cards
    - Encourage pupils, colleagues or parents to collect materials
    - Consult TV and radio programme schedules
    - Write letters to supplying agencies
    - Visit the local Teachers' Centre
    - View in advance any area to be visited later by the class

3. *Prepare the classroom itself*
    - Make a display of related charts, reference books etc.
    - Prepare a display area
    - Prepare resource collections
    - Decide on the layout of furniture
    - Check that any software or apparatus required is readily available
    - Provide suitable folders or storage for pupils' work
    - Organize outside or ancillary help
    - Explore the potential of school-based facilities (such as rain gauges)

As part of planning for environmental topic work the teacher has to be clear about what the children will learn and why. Children always learn *information about* the topic: this might be called *content*. But lesson content is not enough. Infant children are relatively active so they need participatory learning, and a productive way of harnessing this need is to plan which *skills* a child can learn and practise through the pursuit of the topic. Learning is also a cerebral process: it is about thinking. The child's thought processes are expanded and improved through acquisition of *concepts*, and the building up of conceptual structures through which to understand the world in which he or she lives.

Table 24 lists several environmental topics which might prove useful in the infant school. It contains an outline planning grid for each topic of the kind teacher might use to structure her own thinking. Note that in each case the grid is incomplete since the purpose of Table 24 is simply to convey a method of working, not to provide completed topic plans. Examine the methods used in the planning grids and then tackle Task 41.

TABLE 24 Topic planning

TOPIC: MY FAMILY

Content	Skills	Concepts
Who are my family?	Collecting information	Gradual development of the idea of *time*
brothers/sisters		
mum/dad		Conceptual vocabulary: older, younger,
grandparents		before, after,
(and so on)		longer, shorter
What do I know about them?	Asking questions	
When were they born?	Plotting information	(and so on)
What work do they/did they do?	(and so on)	
Where do/did they live? (and so on)		

TOPIC: THE SCHOOL GROUNDS

Content	Skills	Concepts
The playground		
How big is it?	Measuring length	Preparation for the idea of area
What is it made of?		

What games can we play   Inventing
   on it?

The school field
Why do we cut the grass?   Growth and its
How fast does it grow?   preconditions (sun,
                                                           rain)

The school garden
What grows in it?   Close watching

What wild creatures come   Keeping records   Season/weather
   to it?

How often? At what time
   of year?

TOPIC: MY TOWN

Content   ## Skills   ## Concepts

The castle
When was it built?   Finding out from books
Why?
What was daily life like?   Empathizing   Time-span

The cathedral
Built when and by whom?   Spotting styles of
                                building

Why did it take so long?
Why this shape?   Measuring height
How big is it?

The canal
Life on a narrow boat
Narrow boat trip
From where to where?
Who travelled on it and why?

Task 41 Planning an environmental topic of your own

Use the planning methods shown in Table 24 to put together an environmental topic
of your own. When you have completed the outline planning as shown you will need
to get to grips with more detailed issues, eg how you are going to start your topic

off, what variety of teaching methods you are going to use, and how you are going to decide how effectively the children have learned the content, skills and concepts you planned for them. When all this is complete, teach the topic to your class.

Task 42 Judging whether your topic is successful

Finally in this section you should give some thought to whether your topic was successful. To do this you need to establish criteria for judgement. How would you judge success? List your own criteria and then ask several colleagues to do the same. Compare and discuss results. Compile an agreed list. How does your list compare and contrast with that in Table 25?

TABLE 25 Criteria for judging if topic work is successful

A topic is successful if . . .

- the pupils are interested, enthusiastic, motivated and enjoy it
- the quality of work produced is high
- the pupils bring items of interest from home, etc.
- the pupils talk informally about it
- the pupils have gained in knowledge or information
- the pupils' interest is sustained at a high level for a long time
- the pupils can remember the work some weeks/months after it has finished
- good display materials are produced
- the pupils follow the interest outside school or timetable time
- parents comment favourably
- there is a feeling of job satisfaction for the teacher
- the quantity of work done is acceptable/large
- the pupils have acquired and progressed in (unspecified) skills
- the pupils offer ideas and ask questions
- the pupils have gained in experience and understanding
- the teacher's original aims have been fulfilled
- the pupils have produced creative work
- the pupils look forward to topic lessons
- the pupils remember what they have learned
- the topic itself expands in scope spontaneously

Unit 11

AN APPROACH THROUGH SCIENCE

In Unit 10 we argued that children of the infant age group learn experientially and thematically, but that this learning provides them with important tools which form the platform to understanding specific disciplines that are encountered in later life. The concentration in Unit 10 was on sensory experiences, and the same holds true when we consider the relationship of infant curriculum to that discipline we call science. Over the years much ink has been expended, especially in Government Reports and research projects (eg HMI 1978), to try to try to define the place of science in the primary curriculum. Comparatively little of this literature has dealt with the infant age range (but see Harlen 1985). Our view is relatively simplistic but, we believe, pertinent. It can best be explored by taking some common questions about primary/infant science and trying to answer them. The following mock dialogue gives the flavour:

Q: Can children as young as five to seven years fairly be said to 'do science' in any reasonably acceptable sense of the term?

A: The answer must be 'Yes'. A reasonable definition of science in this context would be 'explorations into the world around us, questions and theories about how that world functions, and experiments to see if our ideas or theories work'.

Q: Don't you feel this definition is begging the question?

A: Not at all. This definition, though a little crude, is precisely what scientists have traditionally done. Look back to Galileo, or to Kepler, or to Darwin or to the Reverend Gilbert White. They didn't begin from laboratories, they began from problems in the world about them. When Gilbert White noticed that swallows disappeared in winter and hired village lads to drag the pond to see if they were in hibernation, he was being a scientist. He noticed a puzzle in the natural world, asked the appropriate question, put up an idea (hypothesis, if you prefer), and did an experiment to test it. He was wrong as it happened; but scientists usually are. Few scientific problems are solved at the first attempt.

Q: All right, one could conceive that anyone can, even should, be a scientist in that sense. But isn't studying science in the infant school at such a low level that it's simply re-inventing the wheel, and as such rather time-wasting?

A: That question begs two more by making false assumptions. First, it assumes children of five to seven years cannot discover anything 'new'. It is true that much of what they learn will be new to them perhaps, but not necessarily original to the scientific community. Nevertheless it is *not* impossible for youngsters to make discoveries, albeit simple ones. Take for example the BBC's WATCH project, a naturalist's enquiry in which schoolchildren all over the country collect data. Second, the question assumes that discovering scientific methods and ways of working (eg careful observation and recording) cannot be a valuable starting place in its own right. But surely young people could hardly start anywhere else! And there's another thing. Adults have often become habitual in their thought processes; youngsters bring a vision uncluttered by so many preconceptions . . .

We feel that arguments such as these establish that infant science is worthwhile. Use Task 43 to explore how your colleagues approach this subject area.

Task 43 Exploring the extent and nature of infant science

Try to find an opportunity to talk to about half-a-dozen infants' teachers. Use the questions that follow, augmented by any others you wish to ask, to find out something of the extent and nature of scientific learning in the infant classroom.

- Do your children do any work which you would call scientific or, perhaps, pre-science?
- *If so*, what kinds of things do they do? What content is covered? What skills and concepts do they learn?
- How does this work relate to other curriculum areas which you cover?
- What specific values does this work have for children in this age-range?
- Do you have any particular problem in covering scientific work with infant children?
- *If not*, why do you not tackle work of this nature?

When you have completed your survey based on Task 43 you may have discovered for yourself one very major objection that infants' teachers raise to scientific approaches at this level: 'I am not a scientist'. So is it necessary to be a (trained) scientist, even a gifted amateur one, in order to embark on a scientific approach to learning with infants? The answer is 'No'. But it is necessary to accept particular ways of working with these young children so as to equip them to think and act scientifically. If you prefer you can think of this approach as 'pre-scientific education'. But the fundamentals of it hardly change as the child progresses to what could be termed 'science proper' as he or she gets older.

Pre-scientific education

We might equally have labelled this sub-section: the development of the enquiring mind; because that is precisely what we shall be discussing, and we have hinted at it already in the previous section of this book.

We have already made the point that youngsters whose background experience is not deprived are curious by nature. The teacher's role is to harness that curiosity and to provide the means by which it can be structured while, at the same time, allowing for the child to sustain creative approaches to situations. How might this work in practice? Consider the following scenario:

> Outside the top infants' classroom window is a small garden area and patio. There are roses and buddleia bushes, daisies, and ice plants. They attract butterflies in summer. The children watch with interest as the insects come and go, feeding and lazing on the plants. The teacher engages them in conversation about the insects, about the different colours and patterns. It becomes clear, however, that the children's interest could be exploited further. Not being sure where to go from here, the teacher consults various books on wildlife activities and turns up several suggestions. These are listed after Task 44 below.

Task 44 Judging suitable scientific tasks

Below are seven suggestions for studying butterflies in the school garden. Read them through, and then decide which suggestion(s) you would adopt, *and why.*

The suggestions

1   Find a simple field guide or wall chart guide to British butterflies. Get the children to match the butterflies that they see to plates in the book to identify the species. Concentrate on small details since these are important in naming certain kinds of butterfly (eg the blues).

2   Get the children to look extra carefully at the shapes and patterns of the butterflies. A useful exercise is to encourage the children to draw the butterflies

from life, then to copy their colours. This should be done outdoors for maximum accuracy.

3   The children will notice how the left side of the butterfly is the mirror image of the right. Use this as a starting point for a series of mirror image drawings using everyday objects or natural ones such as leaves. Where applicable, help the children to notice eg whether leaves have a 'mirror image' on either side of the centre vein.

4   Read the children some poems about butterflies such as Aileen Fisher's *Butterfly Tongues*. What do these poems tell us about butterflies and how they live?

5   Encourage the children to ask questions about the behaviour of the butterflies eg which plants do they come to, do all the species come to the same plants, do they feed for as long in dull weather as in sunshine?

6   Find a suitable slide sequence or film strip about the life cycle of the butterfly. Show the children its sequence: egg, caterpillar, chrysalis, insect. Look on your plants for eggs and caterpillars.

7   Having triggered the children's interest in butterfly watching look also for other kinds of insect: greenfly on roses, ants in the grass, dragonflies over a pond.

Now, make the decisions required by Task 44. Only when you have done this, read on.

To tackle the opportunity provided by the butterflies visiting the school garden, within the framework spelled out in the 'pre-scientific enquiry' model outlined above, the teacher would begin by encouraging the children to raise questions and by raising some herself. The most likely are

- What are these butterflies called?
- Why do these feed more on some flowers than others? Which do they feed on most?
- Why are there none here today/lots here today?
- How do butterflies get born?

The pre-scientific enquiry model, then, *encourages children themselves to raise questions* and then to attempt to answer them using their senses (look back to Unit 10 for the importance of senses in infant education). The key activity from the list of seven suggestions would be the fifth; but number five cannot be pursued effectively without number one. The work resulting from one and five combined would almost certainly lead to number six, and could be combined with any of the others (which are all legitimate as far as they go). But it is number five that demands scientific method: observe, ask questions, put forward ideas/guesses/theories, devise experiments, draw conclusions and do it all through careful observation. The teacher in our scenario chose numbers five and one initially, followed by number six. The resulting lessons went roughly as described in the following brief account.

Following the children's obvious interest in the butterflies in the garden the teacher encouraged them to ask questions. They wanted to know what they were called. They noticed that some were white, others brown with coloured patterns, some almost black with red and white marks, and so on. Dawn said there were more butterflies on the ice-plants than on the roses. Tony thought that this might have something to do with the colour of the flowers. Richard thought the white butterflies preferred the long flower-heads of the buddleia and walked about a lot on them. The teacher said she thought that the class should do a project on the butterflies to see if they could check out their observations, but first they would have to find out what the butterflies were called. Back in the classroom they used the time till lunch-time looking at pictures in reference books which the teacher had found. By standing at the windows and checking they decided that their garden housed small whites, tortoiseshells, red admirals and peacocks. The teacher promised that next day they would think out how to plot which butterflies came to which flowers, and how often.

Next day the children came excitedly to the lesson ready to plot their butterflies. The teacher divided the class into four groups. The groups had to watch types of flowers. They had a grid like this. The teacher called these picture grids because the pictures helped the children plot information quickly and accurately.

Group 1 watched the roses, Group 2 the buddleias, Group 3 the ice-plants and Group 4 the daisies. Each time a butterfly landed on their flower type the group would tick the box below the butterfly's picture. The children wanted to rush out and start work, but the teacher showed them they'd get more butterflies to stay if they sat quietly and watched from a distance. They did, and ticked the boxes. Later they looked at the results.

The teacher pointed out that there were fewer small whites in the garden than the other kinds, but the children still spotted some interesting phenomena:

- all the butterflies preferred ice-plants and buddleias to roses or daisies
- red admirals seemed to like ice-plants a lot
- tortoiseshells seemed to like buddleia best
- very few butterflies liked roses

The next day they wanted to do the same thing again, but the teacher pointed out that it was dull so it would be a bit cold outside. Darren looked and said there were no butterflies anyway. They talked about this and decided to do another chart to see if there were more butterflies when it was sunny than when it was dull. The teacher asked for ideas about how to plot this information. They decided to look at the garden at the beginning of break, lunch-time and afternoon break every day the following week. The next week they did this and made a chart like this

MONDAY			TUESDAY			WEDNESDAY			THURSDAY			FRIDAY		
B	L	B	B	L	B	B	L	B	B	L	B	B	L	B

NUMBER OF BUTTERFLIES

7	4	11	3	6	4	0	0	0	2	6	13	2	4	0

WEATHER

☁ Dull

☀ Sun

🌧 Rain

From this chart they discovered that butterflies come to the flowers to feed mainly in the sunshine and not ever when it rains. On Friday Darren found a caterpillar on a stinging nettle leaf when they went out to count and asked the teacher what kind it was. She looked it up and found out it was a tortoiseshell. She decided it was time to give the children an insight into the life cycle of the butterflies, so the following week she brought in some wall-charts they could look at and discuss. When they found out that some of their butterflies were probably breeding in the nettlepatch they got excited and wanted to tell the younger children. The teacher said they should perhaps wait a day or so and prepare a little talk for the six-year-olds on what they had found in the garden, then they could take them to see some of the butterflies if it was sunny.

Now that you have read this account you might like to compare what happened in those lessons with the findings of Wynne Harlen (1985), a scientist who has spent many years investigating aspects of scientific education. She feels that successful scientific learning depends upon providing certain kinds of classroom opportunities for children. Table 26 is based on her conclusions.

 ## Task 45 Judging the scientific approach of a lesson

Look at Table 26. Now look back over the lesson account above. To what extent does this lesson apparently fulfil Wynne Harlen's criteria? Is it successful scientific education? To what extent do you think that you could adopt this approach in your own teaching?

TABLE 26 Criteria for judging the scientific approach of a lesson

The scientific approach is being followed if pupils
- devise their own problems (at least in part)
- understand clearly what they are trying to discover
- trade and discuss ideas or guesses with one another
- devise and use simple tests or experiments
- draw some conclusions from their evidence
- make a record of what they have discovered
- relate the findings to previous knowledge
- reflect on how their tests could be improved

The teacher's approach to infant science can be neatly summarized, then, in a diagram from Harlen and Osborne (1985):

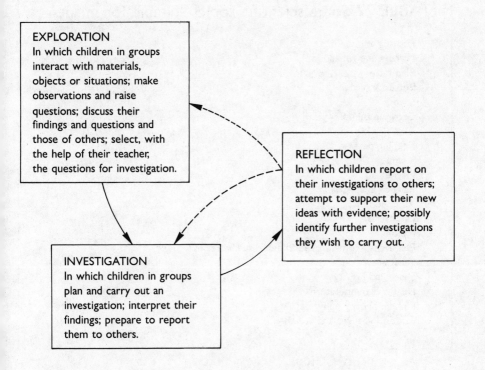

EXPLORATION
In which children in groups interact with materials, objects or situations; make observations and raise questions; discuss their findings and questions and those of others; select, with the help of their teacher, the questions for investigation.

REFLECTION
In which children report on their investigations to others; attempt to support their new ideas with evidence; possibly identify further investigations they wish to carry out.

INVESTIGATION
In which children in groups plan and carry out an investigation; interpret their findings; prepare to report them to others.

So do I have to be a scientist?

The answer is 'Yes'. Every intelligent human being has to be a scientist. We all use the scientific method in one or more contexts every day. One of us might try out a new recipe: domestic science. A new friendship may blossom within the parameters of the behavioural sciences. One of us might try to soup up the car engine: a piece of technological science! And we all try our hand at meteorological science: 'Do you think it'll rain today or shall I leave the washing out?'

For an infants' teacher to follow the scientific method it requires no more and no less expertise than to be a mathematician, to teach reading or language or to treat an historical subject. But it does require, as all teaching requires, for the teacher *to learn at her own level when necessary* in order to pursue a classroom theme effectively. We hope this unit has encouraged you to do just that: to adopt a questioning, problem-solving, experimental (ie a scientific) approach to your classroom teaching. Table 27 sets out some possible subjects that can be pursued in an infant school; but there are plenty more and you should add your own.

TABLE 27 Some scientific topics suitable for infants

Floating and sinking
Mirrors and reflections
Bird table
Butterfly garden
Speed
Growing things
Classification
Keeping pets
Sound
Magnetism
Rainbows and colour
Absorption
Life cycles
Melting
Electricity – simple experiments with batteries
Yeast and baking
Space and gravity
Heat and temperature
Pinhole photography
Seasonal changes and weather

Unit 12

LEARNING THROUGH THE SENSES

'The expressive Arts are universal forms of communication.
Through engaging in them, children develop awareness of themselves as aesthetic and social beings.' (Dankworth 1984)

The potential of music

Teachers generally provide a stimulating environment for the children in their
classes, with respect to sight and touch. Other experiences may be overlooked.
One of the senses which can be educated quite easily is hearing. Sounds are
all around us in the infant school, and with careful structuring they can even
become organised sounds – music!

Children make sounds all the time – they talk, shout, cry, scream or sing.
A good way to focus on sounds is to tell stories needing 'sound effects', such
as those of police cars, ambulances, trains or ghosts. Rhymes and poems can
also be used, and can, for example, help develop good vowel sounds with
pieces like 'On the Ning Nang Nong . . . ' (Herdson 1981, Milligan 1968).
'Sounds Fun' (Wishart 1980) is also a useful source book. The group sits in a
circle, everyone claps three times, then leaves a space (equivalent to three more
claps) then everyone claps three times again. How the gap is filled is up to the
teacher. Herdson suggests 'oohs', then alternately 'oohs' and 'aahs'.

Use of records and tapes

Since we are in the era of what Harold Wilson called 'White-hot technology'
modern aids should be used to the full. So recording tapes and (eventually)
compact discs can play an active part in a music curriculum in many ways:

- Recorded music can provide incentives for movement, playing and painting.
- Recordings can teach you the repertoire of songs, poems and singing games you need. Recordings can also teach children and serve as an accompaniment to their singing.
- Recorded stories leave the teacher free to share the enjoyment of active participation with the children.
- A tape recorder can be used to tape sounds heard around the classroom – the children's experiences with sound and prepared performances (Dankworth 1984).

Television and radio broadcasts

Good use can be made of the excellent television programme, 'Music Time'. The children learn a specific number of songs each term, usually as part of a theme, and some musical notation is introduced. 'Time and Tune' on the radio can also be used to develop an understanding of rhythm.

Rehearsed performances

These are a feature of most schools, especially for festivals such as Christmas, Easter and Mothers' Day. The children prove to have an amazing capacity for learning the words to so many songs! They give excellent experience in singing as a large group and sometimes solo. Such events involve other kinds of learning too, affective skills such as co-operation, self-confidence, or concern for others.

Visiting performers

Visiting performers who produce musical entertainment in the form of musical plays, recitals or larger-scale concerts extend the music in school in a very valuable way, in that the children see the scope of music, and the enjoyment to be gained from it. If such performers cannot be a regular feature of school life (eg because of financial constraints), consider whether you have any musical friends or acquaintances who might be prepared to invest an hour or two in worthwhile work with youngsters.

Task 46 Selecting music for listening

Now that you have thought a little about kinds of musical experience which children might need and enjoy, attempt to build up your own repertoire of music to which children might enjoy listening. Make a card index and possible titles. You might group by theme, or in some other appropriate way. Add to your index whenever you hear something new and appropriate.

Children can gain a great deal of enjoyment from listening to music, but before they do, there are a number of pre-listening activities which will help them understand the 'language' of music through singing, percussion and movement.

Singing

This can take place every day in the infant classroom in short informal sessions. Nursery rhymes are an excellent start. It is a good idea to listen for the children who sing in tune, as some cannot sing in tune until they are about eight years old. Those who sing well can be asked to sing as a group and then individually after a while. The others will benefit from hearing children sing in tune and it is best if they also sit near the teacher where they can be led strongly in the singing so that they can participate and enjoy themselves. Singing sessions are best without percussion at first: although the percussion attracts those few who don't enjoy singing, it may become a distraction, as the children often forget all about quality of singing once instruments appear!

Think about opportunities to sing: could you sing prayers, sing at story-time, compose short songs about any project work in progress to a familiar tune?

Choice of songs

Choice of songs for infants is limitless, but action songs are really excellent, eg 'Five Little Speckled Frogs', 'Five Little Firemen', 'Row Row Your Boat' (the actions give those who don't particularly like singing sessions something to think about!). Where a name can be introduced into the song such as 'Down by the River', the children are very easily involved. They thoroughly enjoy being personalized into the song. *Sing a Song One* is a good compilation of songs for children and is published by Thomas Nelson/ILEA Learning Materials Service.

The teacher can very quickly build up her own repertoire of songs which she enjoys and which she finds useful for the children in her class.

Percussion

Percussion sounds can be produced in a number of ways. Here are some ideas to get you started:

- Body percussion sounds are a good start – the finger click, hand clap, knee pat and foot stamp. The children enjoy using these four body sounds to accompany music or their own songs.
- Percussion instruments or home-made rhythm instruments can then be introduced. The teacher can focus on contrasts – high/low, long/short, soft/loud. Once the children are competent in listening to the pulse of the music, strong/weak beats can be introduced – perhaps with body percussion; pat knees on the accent and click fingers on the weak beats.

With percussion, the child needs to match the sound with the particular instrument, so it must be a good, clear sound. The child needs to know practical skills such as striking a chime bar right in the middle and where to strike a triangle.

Making a 'Sound Corner'

Small rhythm instruments can be produced easily and provide the child with opportunities for experimenting with different sounds: not only different sounds from different 'instruments', but also different sounds from the same instrument – eg different shakers (if the container or the filling differ so will the sound).

The teacher can structure this by one day displaying all the shakers at once. The children can play a game, testing each other on identification of sounds, 'That's the blue shaker' etc.

Task 47 Experimenting with a sound corner

If possible, set up your own 'Sound Corner'; structure it over a period of three days in a similar manner to above and then provide a mixture of instruments on the fourth day. How did the children's experiments with sounds differ on the first three days to the fourth day?

Dankworth suggests the following simple materials and instruments:

- Drums – round plastic fridge containers, tins with tight fitting plastic lids. (Remove base of tin and seal with adhesive tape).
- Gongs – pieces of metal and pottery which can be suspended, then struck to set them vibrating.
- Shakers – containers (of various material, shape and size) with various fillings – seeds, soil, sand, stones, pebbles, peas. (Transparent containers where possible as children are curious as to their contents).

- Jingles – small objects mounted in such a way that they dance and jingle against each other.
- Clappers – two like surfaces clapped together – stones, pebbles, bones, shells, sticks, plastic boxes.
- Scraper – anything with ridges on its surface – notched stick, cheese grater, comb, metal washboard, corrugated cardboard.
- Crackly paper – tissue, cellophane, plastic wrappers, plastic egg boxes, 'bubbly' parcel paper.
- Hearing material – paper and cloth of different textures.
- Water – (on a separate table) containers for pouring, straws and tubes for blowing bubbles, stones for plopping.

Education through movement

The following games focus on movement as part of a response to music.

Children can develop a sense of the underlying pulse in music by listening to records which have consistent pulsation, catchy melody and good instrumentation such as folk dances and songs, some pop songs, nursery rhymes, ballroom dances, Latin-American music, marches and waltzes. The teacher leads the children in a game of 'follow my leader' to the music, using every part of the body in turn: the head – nod, shake, tilt from side to side, roll clockwise, anti-clockwise, develop a 'nervous twitch'! Then eyes – blink, wink, stare etc. Then shoulders, elbows, hands, fingers, hips, legs, knees, feet and toes.

Dankworth suggests work on mime next, to the pulse or the beat of the music: simple mimes such as cooking, household chores, gardening, sport etc. She suggests a variety of speeds of music to change the movements from slow to fast, to medium, to slow and so on.

We also need to explore the potential of movement for self-expression in isolation.

Movement in education has been categorized by Lewis & Cherrington (1984) into three types:

- Action-directed, through efficient body management towards mastery of certain kinds of physical challenge. This leads to gymnastics.
- Trials of strength and speed and movement concerned with projectiles and/or implements. This leads to athletics and sports skills and games.
- Movement emphasising rhythm and phrasing often using sound accompaniment and giving expression to ideas. This leads to dance.

The third category of movement, otherwise known as dance, is the one which appeals to the child through the senses most overwhelmingly. It is important for many reasons, not least that it:

- aids physical development and awareness;
- develops spatial awareness;
- aids personal and social development;
- encourages emotional development.

Although not 'creative', even country dance has a contribution to make to the child's movement experience as it develops a sense of pattern and sequence (and gives enjoyment!) In fact, a child's capacity for movement shows from the earliest times, and as he matures, he gradually gains increased motor control. It has been suggested that a child needs to develop certain physical co-ordination skills before he can attempt particular academic tasks. Psychologists believe that movement activities are a fore-runner of intellectual development, that 'the child uses movement and play in order to learn.' (Lewis and Cherrington, op cit). The movement experiences with which he is provided are obviously very important in these developing years and they must be very carefully planned.

During movement lessons, as the teacher is attempting to appeal to the child through his senses, she can provide a variety of experiences which intermingle:

- Visual experiences – painting, sculpture, pieces of machinery at work, slides or posters of natural elements eg the sea.
- Auditory experiences – music, stories, songs, percussion, poems, rhymes, body percussion sounds.
- Tactile experiences – rough/smooth, wet/dry, warm/cold, spikiness, stickiness etc (bread, dough, clay).

The teacher usually selects relevant experiences to focus on a particular theme; to follow up a visit perhaps, or to extend some project work into a more expressive mode. Perhaps the children have enjoyed a story very much just recently and to develop their understanding and expressive abilities, some of the characters or conditions present in the story – an icy January day for example could act as an excellent stimulus for creative movement!

The diagram in Table 28 below represents some different types of stimuli for movement or dance.

Task 48 Designing activities to develop the senses

Consider either a recent trip which excited your class, or a story which appealed to them. Select an activity incorporating each of the three types of sensory stimulus:
- visual
- auditory
- tactile

Use your chosen activity to form a follow-up session to the trip or story, reinforcing learning and enjoyment through the sensory activity in each case.

Afterwards, talk to the children about their feelings in carrying out these activities and discuss what they think they learned from them.

TABLE 28 Stimuli for music or dance

Sound
percussive words, mouth sounds, electronic music, body sounds

Visual
movement of other children, paintings, sculptures, mobiles, sea, wind, machinery

Literary
an outing, poems, stories

Tactile
roughness, smoothness, sharpness, spikiness, malleability, stickiness (bread, dough, clay)

Unit 13

THE CONCEPTUAL BASIS OF THE INFANT CURRICULUM

Traditionally the work of English schools has been content-led. To draw up a curriculum meant to list the information to be taught under a number of subject headings. Popular mythology at any rate believes that this is because all school work has led to and been dominated by the former GCE examination, which demanded recall knowledge only. It will be interesting to see whether the advent of GCSE changes the education world's thinking on the issue! Though the infant curriculum has been least affected by this kind of thinking it remains true that most teachers would find it hard to give a secure reply to questions like:

- What are the major cognitive goals of infant education?
- How are these met through curriculum planning?
- What, indeed, should a child learn between four-and-a-half and seven years of age?
- How can the success of this learning be measured?

But it has to be said that these are the really fundamental kinds of question that need to be asked about all education, and it is in answering these questions that teachers become genuinely accountable in professional terms. Since schools in this country have so much curriculum freedom it is crucial that individual teachers can answer these questions effectively. It is about these aspects of your teaching that we shall ask you to think more carefully in this Unit.

Task 49 Exploring the basis of the infant curriculum

Ask two or three colleagues if they are willing to be interviewed about how they decide what to teach and how, ie the curriculum of their classroom. Spend about half an hour with each person. Use the questions that follow as a guide, but add your own as necessary to clarify anything which you would like them to elaborate. Make notes as you proceed. When you have conducted the interviews try to draw conclusions about how curriculum is planned and on what basis.

TABLE 29 Planning guide: interviewing colleagues about curriculum issues

1   At the beginning of the academic year, how do you decide what to teach for the next twelve months? Who else is involved in this decision-making?

2   In making these decisions what factors condition your thinking (eg ground pupils have already covered, reports sent on by a previous teacher)?

3   This year, for example, what progress would you expect children in your class to have made by next July?

       What new content/information will they have acquired?
       What new skills will they have gained?
       What new concepts will they have understood?

4   How will you decide upon the teaching methods you are going to use during the year?

5   Do you try to take stock, at the beginning of the year, what knowledge, skills, and understanding the children already have? How do you do this?

6   At the end of the year what information will you pass on to the children's next teacher/their junior school?

Content, skills and concepts

Quite major research studies into primary schools have revealed that curriculum planning is sometimes quite haphazard and arbitrary. Consider the following research findings culled from various sources.

- School A has no curriculum statement or policy.
- The head of school B delegates curriculum decisions to year group leaders.
- Teachers in school C are free to opt out of any curriculum decisions made by the year-group leader if they feel out-of-tune with them.
- Every teacher in school D makes unilateral curriculum decisions.

- Teacher X in school E decided last week to do 'The Romans' because there is a television series scheduled for the autumn term. She is hoping it will be interesting.

These examples are typical rather than isolated examples of curriculum planning methods employed in primary schools. We even met one headteacher in a rural school (head plus just one staff member) who said curriculum decisions were made by her staff member and she followed suit because 'It saves the nervous problems of managerial conflict'. The examples cited are not extreme cases, and one or other of them (or some equivalent) probably occurs in four schools out of every ten at the primary level. So how can we improve on the situation?

Since it is clear that many curriculum decisions come down to the individual class teacher *the obvious line of attack is initially to make every teacher an effective curriculum planner.*

So far in this book we have taken the view that there are three aspects to curriculum planning. The teacher has to consider:

- the *content* the children need to know
- the *skills* they need to acquire
- the *concepts* they need to understand.

We have suggested, however, that the real impetus of learning relates to the third of these, understanding concepts. It is, then, our view that curriculum planning has to *begin* with concepts, or better still with concepts coupled with skills, and that suitable content can be hung flesh-like over this crucial skeletal structure of concepts-skills without which all learning would collapse. One or two examples illustrate the theme. Let us assume that a suitable concept for infants to understand is 'care'.

> Teacher A decides to tackle this through the children's interest in pets. So the children are taught how to look after the pet rabbit in the classroom, how to keep it clean, feed and water it, and how it needs care in holiday time, too. So they form a holiday rota.
>
> Teacher B uses story-time to tell a series of stories with a caring theme: the five loaves and the fishes, St Francis, Dr Barnardo.
>
> Teacher C gets the children to put on a carol concert for old folk living alone, along with some biscuits and tea made by the children themselves.

All of the approaches outlined are legitimate activities directed at the same basic understanding of the concept 'care'. The content of work has been different in each case but the learning has been to the same end: it is the understanding which is primary. The same kind of insight holds true of skills. On page 106 we described a piece of work on butterflies which began from children looking at insects outside the classroom window. The work required the children to record and report findings: they learned to use picture-grids, and they gave a talk to another class. These recording and reporting skills are basic to all scientific learning (and also to other areas). But precisely the same skills could have been acquired as a result of a traffic survey, a review of favourite television programmes or a review of prices in the local sweet shop. Skill acquisition is of more lasting significance than the detailed content or information which forms the vehicle through which the learning takes place.

If our view is correct, that decisions about concepts and skills need to take precedence over content decisions, then most curriculum planning in contemporary primary schools begins at the wrong end of the process! Assuming that we are correct, the next question is: why? The answer, we believe, lies in expediency. For the average teacher, curriculum decisions are easier and planning is therefore quicker if the starting point is content. It is easier to answer the question 'What shall I do with the children?' than to explore the problem 'What concepts/skills do my five/six/seven-year-olds need to acquire this year, and how can I best put these across?' The second approach is harder, but we believe, more effective. It is to tackling this issue that we devote most of the rest of Unit 13.

Identifying concepts and skills for the infant curriculum

Before embarking on this sub-section the time has come for you to take stock of your own curriculum planning. Task 50 gives you the opportunity to do this.

Task 50 Reviewing your own curriculum planning

Take a long, hard look at the material you have planned to teach for the next term. (If you are a student-teacher you may have to use the material relating to your last or next teaching practice). Answer honestly the questions below.

- How exactly did you decide on this curriculum material?
- Are you satisfied with the criteria on which you based those decisions? If not, why not?
- Can you identify clearly the *concepts* and the *skills* which your curriculum conveys? In each case list them.
- What criteria/methods were used to assess whether the children had *understood* the *concepts* and *acquired* the *skills* you intended?
- How does the work in this curriculum block relate to things they learned beforehand and to things that will come after?

- Are you satisfied that these relationships forward and back are logical, and that they fit into an overall curriculum strategy?
- Can you set out in a paper or two the outline of this curriculum strategy for the infant years?

Now that you have had a chance to scrutinize your own curriculum planning skills we need to address the rather wider set of issues about a curriculum strategy for the infant years in more detail.

Let us begin with the conceptual basis of infant education. The crunch question is: can we actually identify concepts that infants need to (begin to) acquire and which are fundamental to this age-range for all children? What we need is a kind of concept bank or conceptual map on which to draw. Since the issue is open to some debate let us look at the different but related approaches of two schools that have tried to come to terms with this issue. Tables 30 and 31 set out kinds of planning which inform curriculum decisions in these schools.

Task 51 Deciding on your own conceptual map for infant education

With the leads provided by Tables 30 and 31 have another look at your own work. If you are a class teacher, take your curriculum plan for the year and re-write it setting out the key concepts you have taught or plan to teach. When you have finished, review the concepts and decide whether any are superfluous or repeated unnecessarily, and whether there are any gaps in your provision. (If you are a student teacher this exercise might be useful to you if you simply use the age-group you expect to be teaching next as the one around which to plan. Headteachers using this material could try to make an all-through conceptual map for the school).

Now that you have decided which concepts are important for your age-group you should try to work out which skills are implicit in them, and which other skills are relevant to your age-group. For example

Concept	*Implicit Skills*
Area (of square, rectangle)	Ability to measure accurately with a ruler
	Ability to multiply two simple numbers correctly

TABLE 30 The conceptual basis of infant education at Rosewood School (extract)

The properties of water

Content	Skills	Concepts and activities	Methods and resources
Water Pressure	Observation using all senses.	*Water Pressure* The force of water, pouring water onto a tray of sand, raised at one end. Water finding its own level – pouring water into a plastic tube.	Each area of content to be undertaken by all the class working in small groups, through a series of experiments.
	Recording using a variety of methods including oral.		
Clean and polluted water	Classifying using	*Clean and polluted water* Filtering water to find impurities. Boiling water to find impurities. Repeating processes using salt water. Dissolving soil, sugar, salt and sand in water. Saturated solutions.	
	appropriate means		
	Emphasis on accuracy		
	Pupil's conclusions rather than teachers'		
	Simple prediction		
	Measurement		

Content	Skills	Concepts and activities	Methods and resources
Floating and sinking	Observation using all senses. Recording using a variety of methods including oral.	*Floating and sinking* Guessing which of a collection of objects will float. Testing earlier predictions – finding things that float. Floating under control. Why do some things float? Measuring objects in air and water. Floating below the surface. Floating in salt water.	Each area of content to be undertaken by all the class working in small groups, through a series of experiments.
	Classifying using appropriate means.		
Evaporation	Emphasis on accuracy. Pupil's conclusions rather than teacher's.	*Evaporation* Observation of clouds – Drawing a cloudy day picture. Observation of a puddle – looking for evaporation. Evaporation in different environments. Measuring evaporation. Slowing down evaporation – jars with and without lids.	
Condensation	Simple prediction. Measurement.	*Condensation* Condensation of steam on a cold surface. Water vapour – sentence completion task. Condensation – using jar of ice.	
Water cycle		*Water cycle* Drawing of diagram to represent water cycle. Filmstrip to explain, simply, the water cycle.	Filmstrip.

TABLE 31 The conceptual basis of infant education at Hawthorn School

(Extract from staff handbook)

Concepts

A concept is a general idea which represents a group of things, actions or relationships, having certain characteristics in common. (e.g. fruit, mountain, market.)

Some concepts are quite simple whilst others are more complex. It is important that we teach concepts for several reasons. Firstly because to attempt the teaching of facts only would be futile. Facts are so numerous that to teach them all would be impossible, the number of facts increases daily and can soon become out of date. Secondly, children develop a growing store of concepts which help them to understand and interpret new situations and experiences as they arise. Thirdly, concepts act as organisers and summaries for us when meeting new experiences and finally they are anchor points in learning to which the teacher will want to return from time to time in order to stress their role in learning.

In Integrated Studies three concepts have been identified which are common to History, Geography, Science and most of the primary school curriculum. They are:-

Similarity / Difference
Continuity / Change
Cause / Consequence

These three concepts are concerned with ways of classifying and examining subject-matter.

Similarity / Difference is obviously concerned with classifying. Continuity /Change can be used to examine Then and Now or even Then and Then through the study of the same place at different times. Cause and consequence arise through the need to consider why some things differ from others and why things change.

It is not expected that the children will be able to grasp those concepts although it may be possible in some cases that children will become able to use and begin to understand the actual terms.

The main use of these three concepts is for teachers in planning topics. Their use will enable teachers to examine possible content in a selective way so that the content can be 'pruned' to that which is relevant and meaningful and contains a relatively coherent progression in concept development.

It has been a common practice in topic planning to draw up a topic 'web'. For example, a possible topic web on 'Canals' may look like this –

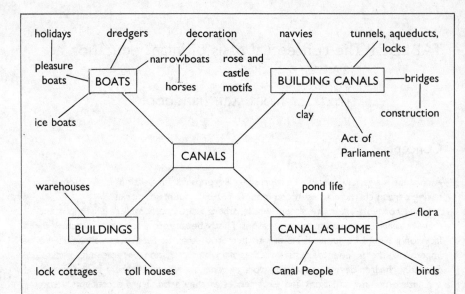

This topic web concerns itself only with those things related to 'Canals' and all of the content in it is related to that topic. It would be possible to develop the web much further including many more items which, it could be argued, would be related to the topic of 'Canals'. Yet it would be difficult to show a purposeful relationship between 'bridge construction' and 'water birds' or 'holidays'.

Alternatively, the three concepts can be used as 'organisers' around which the content can be grouped. This has the effect of pruning and limiting the content to those items which are relevant and purposeful. Furthermore, when the concepts have been used in the planning of content, it should be certain that what is taught is conceptually based and that those concepts will be continuously developed.

The content for 'Canals' organised in this way may look like this:-

SIMILARITY/DIFFERENCE
Canal Home/Land Home
Canal Art
Canal flora/alternative habitat

CAUSE/CONSEQUENCE
Poor roads/Canal Development
Coming of railways/
    decline of canals
Canal buildings
Locks, aqueducts,
    tunnels, bridges
Building problems

CONTINUITY/CHANGE
Canals past and present
Boat types

Task 52 Adding skills to concepts in the curriculum

Take several large sheets of paper. You are going to draft a curriculum plan on these. Divide the paper vertically into five columns of equal width. In the left-hand column (column one) list the concepts which you have decided are crucial to the work of your class (or school). Leave yourself plenty of space between each item in the list as you go down the column. Now in column two write in, opposite each concept, the skills the children will need or acquire in coming to understand it. In the third column you can now begin to compile suggestions for the content through which these concepts and skills can be learned. You will now have a grid that looks something like this:

A curriculum for 6-7-year-olds				
Concepts	Skills	Content		

Keep your chart as we shall go back to it in the next Task.

At this stage, if you have carried out Tasks 51 and 52, you will have discovered what precisely you hope the children will learn while they are in your care. By now you will have a pretty good idea of what learning experiences you will have to provide, and what roles you will have to play. For example, if you want the children to learn the skill of feeling and weighing in order to gain an understanding of the concept 'heavier', you will need to set up the work in a problem-solving manner, using appropriate apparatus. You will be the arbiter of the child's judgement. Perhaps you will also teach discrimination through practice of motor and sensory skills. These teaching methods and teacher roles are as important to curriculum planning as is the identification of the concepts, the skills or the content. Teaching method needs to be both *appropriate* and *varied* in order to ensure effective learning and to sustain children's enthusiasm. With this in mind you can proceed to Task 53.

Task 53 Deciding upon teaching methods

Go back to the curriculum plan on which you have compiled three columns and complete the fourth: teaching methods.

What have the children learned?

So we come to the last column of the concept-based curriculum planner which you have been compiling. You have decided upon the key concepts for your chosen group of children, and have added to these the skills required so that the youngsters can aquire and practise them. You have indicated some suitable content through which these concepts and skills can be learned, and chosen appropriate teaching methods. Let us assume you have taught, or are about to teach, this material. Now you need to know in what ways you intend to measure whether the children have indeed understood the concepts, acquired the skills and remembered some of the information. In each case you need to decide how these things can be tested. Some examples of this evaluation procedure would be:

- Asking feedback questions generally of the class.
- Questioning an individual child in depth.
- Getting a child or group to recount their learning to another.
- Setting a similar task to test application.
- Asking for a judgement, with reasons: 'Which is heavier? Why do you think so?'
- Encouraging a child to read a paragraph *fluently and with expression*.

Task 54 Evaluating learning

Add column five's heading to your curriculum planner: evaluation procedures. Now complete column five.

On completion of all the reading and activities in Unit 13 of this book you should have a firm grasp of the basic principles of sound curriculum planning in the infant school. There are just a few more points upon which you might like to reflect.

First, if it is in accord with your school policy, you should be ready and able to explain curriculum decisions to parents of pupils in your class. Most parents take an active interest in their youngsters' work, but many do not understand much about school work and have outmoded ideas about what goes on in school. Those who do understand schools will be especially appreciative to know that you have tackled your job in a thoughtful and accountable way.

Second, if you are in a managerial role or aspire to one, you really should consider the implications for curriculum planning across the whole school. The English education system allows scope for curriculum freedom, but this freedom must be tempered by a management responsibility to see that *all* children within the school are learning effectively. How exactly heads, deputies or year group leaders tackle this issue will depend in part upon management style. But tackled it must be! Moves by LEAs in recent years (eg the Salford LEA's Profile 82) are clearly a step in the right direction.

Third, some teachers protest that curriculum planning of the kind advocated here is mechanistic and is insufficiently child-centred for an infant school. Actually, this is nonsense. Clearly children cannot take a professional overview of their own curriculum needs: the method described here is designed to do just that. The method – which is one for long-term planning – in no way precludes instant response on a day-to-day basis to precisely what children need and show interest in. By adopting a concept-led planning procedure it may actually free teachers to pursue content of more immediate excitement to children for, as we have seen, specific content is no longer central to the learning process. If you glance back at the brief lesson description on page 106 for example, you will note that it was the *children's* interest which the teacher encapsulated as a medium through which to think and plan vigorously for concepts and skills. At first, thinking out the curriculum in this professionally rigorous way is difficult; but it soon becomes second nature. Just a little effort is all that is required initially, though it is this which (one suspects) some teachers find hard to make. If all teachers at all phases of the education system were to adopt this approach the quality of education would rise: and would do so without a massive increase in time and labour and without a Government subsidy. By being strict about introducing the evaluation stage it would also give teachers an instant measure of their 'productivity'.

Finally it should be noted that the first thirteen sections of this book have dealt substantially with what might be regarded as the content of infant education: curriculum issues, how to tackle curriculum planning, and traditional curriculum areas. What follows in the next six Units changes the emphasis to specific aspects of teaching skill. Unit 13 was, in effect, a transition section from one approach to the other. It is really only a difference of viewpoint; but it is one which we believe will be helpful in developing teachers who are all-round, effective and thinking professionals.

Unit 14

TRACKING AND RECORDING PUPILS' PROGRESS

In this Unit we will address ourselves to five main considerations:

- What should the teacher record?
- How should she record it?
- For whom are the records kept?
- For what purpose are the records kept?
- How can continuous assessment promote progress?

Consider the following quotation:

> 'Most first school teachers carry in their heads a wealth of information about their young charges . . . and often there is no opportunity for them to quantify it.' (Moyles 1986)

Some teachers argue that relationships between teacher and pupil should remain at the *intuitive* rather than *clinical* level, and should therefore go unrecorded. It can be seen however that behavioural *patterns* can become apparent if isolated incidents are carefully recorded. No teacher needs to be told that a child displaying behavioural problems can be as disruptive and disturbed as a child with particular academic problems (which, by contrast, are generally recorded as a matter of course).

In fact if a child is allowed to pass from teacher to teacher through the school exhibiting behaviour problems, and these are not recorded, no pattern will emerge and the child's maladjustment will simply deepen. The teacher will remain without help from other agencies and support services, help which would certainly have been sought earlier had the child's progress, or lack of it, been noted from the beginning. Record-keeping can, then, pin-point the need for the assistance of outside agencies, provided it contains information not only concerning academic progress in all curriculum areas, but also personality traits, motivation and attitudes. Our argument is that record-keeping needs to be on a wider basis than the purely academic in order to be genuinely useful.

Task 55 Identifying legitimate areas about which to keep records

In the light of what has been said above set out a list of those aspects of a child's performance and progress you think are legitimate subjects for record-keeping.

Profiling is a form of record keeping which encompasses all the above considerations. In addition to providing valuable information for a wider audience (eg Reading Advisory Service, Educational Psychologist etc) profiling can:

- provide the teacher with an excellent means of self-evaluation;
- promote pupils' progress by pointing out weaknesses, strengths, omissions etc;
- raise the teacher's awareness of how successful she is in achieving the objectives for the individuals and groups she teaches, both short and long term. Thus, if a whole group of children appear to find difficulty in one particular area, it would suggest to the teacher that she needed to evaluate her own personal contribution: perhaps there was inappropriate or insufficient reinforcement of the topic in question, or she could need to evaluate her classroom organisation.
- promote pupils' progress (this can be done in a variety of ways, which we will explore later in setting out a practical format for class records and profiling).

Let us first of all explore the value of records in tracking the progress of, and helping, slow learners. In discussing record-keeping for this group of pupils Bell and Kerry (1982) suggest that, from time to time, very detailed records of appropriate individuals are made over a period of about three weeks. What kinds of information would be included in such a regular in-depth study?

Task 56 Devising a record proforma for slow learners

Devise your own record-keeping sheet or proforma to take stock and monitor the progress of a group of slow learners in your class. When you have done this, compare your proforma with the headings in Table 32.

TABLE 32 A record-keeping proforma

Pupil's name (or code):
Reading age (if known):
School progress in subjects other than your own:

Results of any diagnostic or assessment tests:

Social strengths or problems:
Emotional strengths or problems:
Academic progress over a three week period:

- in concentration span;
- in language skills;
- in subject specific learning;
- in handling written materials;
- in following instructions;
- in completing classroom tasks.

The table above is detailed and may appear inapplicable to the majority of your class. Yet the 1981 Education Act stated 18% of children in schools have some form of special educational needs. If identification of all the slow learners or those with differing educational needs is difficult, class records and profiling as set out below make the identification simpler, and will more accurately pinpoint their problems.

Keeping effective class records

Most teachers like to keep personal class records of basic achievement by all pupils in the class. They have obvious uses

- as feedback to the teacher
- to inform the head or other staff
- to inform parents when discussing an individual child.

Naturally the material in these records is confidential but they are a valuable source of guidance and a memory bank for the teacher. In the paragraphs that follow one particular scheme, based on Moyles (1986) is outlined. Each teacher, given her own circumstances, really needs to adapt a basic model such as this one.

Moyles suggests the use of matrices which cross reference the child's name to a set of skills.

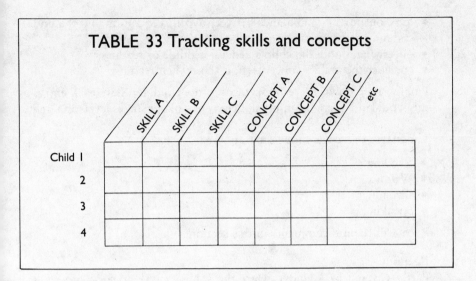

TABLE 33 Tracking skills and concepts

The teacher ticks the appropriate box *when the child acquires the skill or concept involved*, not when the area has been covered. This kind of fairly mechanistic record-keeping is best augmented by a more open system of profiling.

Profiles

Moyles divides her profile into 12 sections as follows:

1 **Personal details**: name, date of birth, address, position in family; date of entering nursery and school; admission number.

2 **Records passed on**: eg from nursery school. These would usually include details of skills acquired (motor skills, social skills, aesthetic skills), and any development in language and number. Hopefully there would also be comments concerning progress made, friendships made and valuable notes concerning the child's adjustment to school life.

3 **Reading**: as Moyles notes, it is 'important to discover the child's strengths and interests, when often only difficulties and weaknesses are noted'. This is the essence of profiling.

   In this section, comments need to describe the child's reading attainment and habits at regular intervals. Reading attainment tests can be used, but need to be supplemented by observation in normal reading situations. Diagnosis *needs* to be a continuing process so that the changing needs of the child are appropriately reflected in his work. In any 'normal' reading situation,

- look out for any imbalance between word recognition and the understanding of what has been read;
- observe and note the child's general attitude to reading;
- consider the child's concentration span when reading.

Finally, note down every book read by the child and date each entry, as this would make lengthy intervals between books or stages/levels apparent.

4   **Language**: this covers four separate areas.

- Reading
- Writing
- Listening
- Speaking

Each will require comments in this section.

Reading
Partly covered in 3, above. Here the teacher needs to focus on specific skills eg phonics (if that is the particular method of teaching reading in her school); in other words, word attack skills. These records need to be extremely detailed as set out in the example in Table 34.

TABLE 34 Recording reading skills: a phonic approach

1	Initial letters	f g h .... etc.
2	Vowels	a e i .... etc.
3	Blends	fr cl .... etc.
4	Word endings	mp ck .... etc.
5	Doubled consonants	tt mm .... etc.
6	Vowel digraphs...	
7	Magic 'e'	

Each separate section in Table 34 will need to be ticked and dated when the child knows all the sounds.

Writing
This will require comments on the child's progress through

- name tracing/pattern tracing on paper or in sand etc;
- name writing;
- writing of captions underneath the teacher's own writing to describe child's own pictures;
- caption writing unaided;
- writing a sentence using a sentence maker or word book and a few memorised words;

- writing a few lines after a stimulus or concerning own experiences;
- fluent writing;
- handwriting practice.

Listening
Make notes on the child's listening skills when

- listening to a story
- listening to the teacher – and responding to questions asked
- listening to other children (a very difficult task for some children, to remain quiet in a discussion when another child is speaking)
- performing audio/visual tasks, eg use of a synchrofax machine
- watching tv programmes at school – level of recall

Speaking
- Note the difference in the fluency of speech between speaking to another child and speaking to you the teacher (if any is discernible).
- Note how the child responds to a wider audience than one-to-one.
  eg: telling a story to the class or group
        playing a part in a class production or small play or assembly.
- Note any differences between the child's speaking ability, reading ability and writing ability.

5   **Mathematics**: all the topics covered by the child will need to be detailed and the level of attainment in each one must be noted. Otherwise, when repeated, the topic may not be covered at the right level. An example is given in Table 35. Levels in the maths scheme employed by the school must be recorded eg Scottish Primary Maths Scheme, Fletcher, Peak etc.
      Open ended comments can be made here, regarding particular areas of strength or interest etc.
Less detailed, but nevertheless, important, sections are concerned with progress in

6   **Scientific / environmental studies**;
7   **Music;**
8   **Moral and religious education;**
9   **Aesthetic development.**
Using the guidelines provided at appropriate units in this book you can now compile your own specific patterns for recording under these headings.

10 **General**: Although open-ended comments have been compiled in the particular areas 1–9 already described, this section gives the teacher the opportunity to draw together all her thoughts to complete the 'whole picture' of the child. Moyles suggests a checklist of the kind shown in Table 36.

TABLE 35 An example of recording mathematical progress

Arbitrary measurement   *Date*

Hand spans   ☐

Feet   ☐

Sticks   ☐

Boxes   ☐

String   ☐

Measuring card   ☐

Standard Measurement

Metre   ☐

Centimetre   ☐

TABLE 36 An example of a general proforma

	Year 1			Year 2			Year 3		
	Terms			Terms			Terms		
	1	2	3	1	2	3	1	2	3
PERSISTENCE capacity for work									
perseverence									
concentration									
memory									
behaviour etc									

11 **Tests**: this section simply requires details concerning tests administered by the teacher or outside agencies, eg Educational Psychologist, Reading Advisory Service teacher, hearing service etc, with dates and results.

12 **Open Comments**: the teacher needs to note down significant points concerning progress and possibly any family problems or health problems which could affect the child's progress and/or personality traits. This will

complete the picture and provide the next teacher in the same school, or in a different school (Junior department or transfer school) with a total progress report.

Samples of the child's work should be placed in the appropriate sections to further illustrate development, each term (as each section requires completion once a term).

Taking stock of record-keeping

Perhaps record-keeping seems to be a long and arduous process, and we have all met teachers who say: 'I carry all the information in my head anyway.' But it is obvious that effective and professional records for over thirty children cannot be kept in the head, although a good teacher will retain a great deal of the information for spur-of-the-moment recall.

Our survey of record-keeping has not been exhaustive. With this in view you might like to try Task 57. You might want to add to your records, for example, something about the teaching methods experienced by each of the children in your class. Has each child taken part in a whole-class lead lesson, worked in a group, regularly followed individualized tasks, experienced co-operative and competitive learning situations (*both* occur in the real world), and so on?

Task 57 Augmenting Moyles' record-keeping system

Look back over this Unit, in particular over the paragraphs dealing with keeping effective class records. What additional information would you keep as part of your own recording system? List the information and use it as part of the next Task.

Task 58 Devising a personal record-keeping system

For the last Task in this Unit you should think about devising your own recording system related to your needs. Using the ideas generated in the text and any thoughts of your own, tailor a recording system or proforma to meet your own needs.

Earlier in this Unit we suggested that record-keeping had particular relevance in diagnosing the problems of slow learners. Unit 15 of this book indicates the need to track the progress of bright pupils. You have just devised a proforma relating to the whole class and ability range. Such diagnostic procedures highlight the individuality and special needs of all pupils, and are crucial to effective task-setting in the infant school. Only by knowing what the needs of the pupils are collectively and individually, can a teacher really begin to meet those needs.

Unit 15

BRIGHT PUPILS AND SLOW LEARNERS

Most teachers can tell almost intuitively that some children in their classes are potentially slow learners and that others are exceptionally able. Research suggests that the judgement is made less on intuition, in reality, and more because of certain tell-tale signs or cues. To take one or two obvious examples, brief concentration span may be an instant cue to a slow learner, and extensive vocabulary may be a signal that a pupil is bright. Individually these cues can be misleading, but cumulatively they tend to aid identification. A checklist of such cues to bright pupils compiled by teachers in secondary schools contained in the following items:

A PROFILE OF THE BRIGHT PUPIL

Criteria
is able to grasp concepts/experiments
has ability to think out problems
shows above average ability
thinks and understands quickly
is able to ask intelligent questions

uses his own initiative
relates new work to previous knowledge
is able to draw conclusions
assimilates facts quickly
has lively, enquiring mind
shows understanding
is able to develop ideas
asks questions beyond what is being taught
puts forward ideas from his own knowledge
is perceptive
is able to answer questions
is able to work alone
is alert
produces good ideas
is quick to react
is willing to learn

Task 59 Identifying bright pupils and slow learners

1 Choose at least half a dozen colleagues and put this question to them:
'Most teachers faced with a new class will quickly spot able pupils. What cues do you use to identify these pupils in a class you haven't met before?'

2 Try to elicit at least three and up to six items from each colleague. Now you will be able to start to see patterns emerging. Make a list of these cues in rank order according to whether they were mentioned 6, 5, 4 (etc) times or only once. *Do not prompt or put suggestions to the respondents* as you will bias your investigation.

3   Using your initial findings, try to compile your own checklist of cues to bright pupils by extending your enquiries to colleagues and by using your own experience.

4   Repeat the experiment perhaps with a new sample of colleagues, this time asking about slow learners instead of bright pupils. Compile your resulting checklist of cues to slow learners.

5   Compare your checklist with the one given below:

TABLE 37 Classroom cues to slow learners from Bell and Kerry (1982)

teachers recognise slow learners as the pupils who . . .

- need specially clear, step by step, repeated instructions
- need extra explanations of subject matter
- need constant extra help
- have reading difficulties
- lack concentration
- have difficulty in comprehension
- do not absorb information
- have writing difficulties
- are easily distracted
- lack basic knowledge or skills
- do work of poor quality
- are slow workers and slow to respond
- are easily confused

Special educational needs

Since the Warnock Report (1978), and above all since the 1981 Education Act came into force, there has been an increasing emphasis on the concept of special educational needs. So far in this Unit we have talked in simplistic terms about bright pupils and slow learners. But it is clear that children cannot in fact be pigeon-holed quite as neatly and compactly as this. The concept of special need attempts to refine our view of brightness and, more especially, of the traditional view of the slow learner. Take a simple example: a teacher notes that a six-year-old is failing to make normal progress in reading. Any of the following, singly or in combination, could be factors in this lack of progress:

- defective eyesight;
- poor hearing;

- home background inimical to books;
- parents who are non-readers;
- immature emotional development;
- temporary emotional crisis;
- lengthy absence in early schooling;
- innately low intelligence level;
- undiagnosed ill-health;
- poor sleeping habits resulting in undue fatigue.

There are three major implications from this list. The first is that it is crucial for the teacher to make a reasonably accurate *diagnosis* of the problem if the child is to be helped effectively. Second, since every class is likely to have several children with special learning needs among its number, the teacher has to evolve ways of coping that imply conscious *teaching strategies* aimed at giving some individual attention to these and to all pupils. Finally, some children's needs will turn out to need very specialist attention, from a doctor, a social worker or through 'statementing' by the LEA under the terms of the 1981 Act. In these cases the teacher must seek early *specialist advice*, via the headteacher, and must not act alone.

The concept of special need tends to be directed towards children with barriers to learning; but actually most children with normal or above average physical and mental abilities may – even if only temporarily – develop special needs. Thus a very bright child may need books that are more advanced than those normally kept in the school; or a child of normal learning ability may suddenly lose interest because of a trauma in his or her home life: an accident, death, illness or divorce. Many schools appoint one teacher as a specialist co-ordinator to provide staff with support in this area: and those co-ordinators are most effective who view their role most widely.

Task 60 Reviewing special needs in your own classroom

Take a list of the pupils in your own class. Go through the list and pick out all those children whom you think have special needs. Take each selected pupil in turn and work out the following:
- the apparent nature of the problem;
- what additional information you need about this child;
- how you can obtain this information;
- what teaching strategies you can adopt to help meet this child's needs;
- what records of progress you need to keep on this pupil;
- with whom you need to liaise about this pupil's needs.
Put your plans into action as soon as possible. Review both the class and your plans once a term.

Testing

So far in this Unit it has been implied that much of the diagnosis and assessment of special needs in the infant school can be done by sensitive teachers using normal powers of professional observation. This is probably true for a majority of the time. Unless it is contrary to specific local policies it is useful to test from time to time also. At the infant level, group tests of intelligence are not helpful; so individual tests need to be found. Several tests are quite helpful, and these include Goodenough's Draw a Man Test (Slough, NFER), Brimer & Dunn's (1962) British Picture Vocabulary Scale (also from NFER), and A. Bachm's Test of Basic Concepts (New York: Psychological Corporation 1970). An interesting new test is the Bury Test (1985) which is relatively simple for a teacher to use. You might also like to look back to Unit 6 and note that some of the reading tests noted there are helpful, too. Quite often it is the *combination* of testing and trained observation which comes up with the most reliable data.

Helping bright pupils

Once you have discovered that one or more of the youngsters in your charge is bright then this will force you to think out exactly how you present material generally and to that child in particular. Chris Burke (in Kerry 1983) has some interesting views on what opportunities should be given to children in primary classes who show ability. These include:

- tackling more demanding work;
- working independently of the teacher;
- developing their own areas of interest;
- working at their own pace when possible;
- being encouraged in creative solutions;
- being encouraged in imaginative work;
- forming simple hypotheses;
- testing their ideas and theories;
- being allowed to ask a lot of questions;
- being asked to make judgments;
- being given appropriately demanding resource materials;
- being asked to argue and reason logically.

Not all able children are keen to be identified as such and some, whom we shall label here as underachievers, resist identification. The motives for this are various, but often come down to social pressure. In other words, bright children may appear to be liked by adults and may thus inspire aggression in other children. To spot these youngsters the teacher will need to work extra hard, looking for tell-tale signs such as the following:

- antagonism to school;
- abrasive humour;
- good oral work but poor or unfinished writing;
- good understanding married to boredom or lethargy;
- susceptibility to distractions;
- emotional insecurity;
- astuteness in reasoning but defensive of shortcomings;
- friendship with older children or adults rather than peer-group.

To develop the thinking of able pupils teachers need to plan work so that it will make genuine cognitive demands on them. The following diagram based on the *Guide to Science 5–13 'With objectives in mind'* (Schools Council 1980) gives an indication of how this can be achieved:

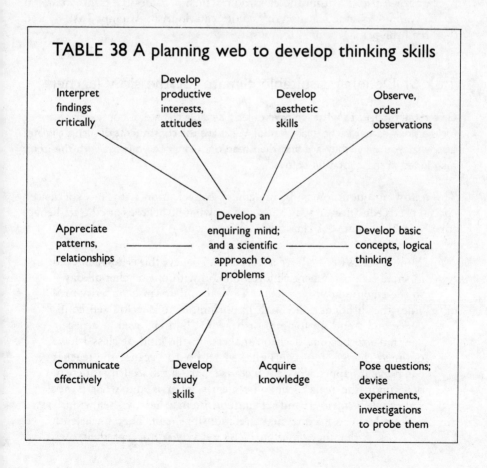

TABLE 38 A planning web to develop thinking skills

Interpret findings critically

Develop productive interests, attitudes

Develop aesthetic skills

Observe, order observations

Appreciate patterns, relationships — Develop an enquiring mind; and a scientific approach to problems — Develop basic concepts, logical thinking

Communicate effectively

Develop study skills

Acquire knowledge

Pose questions; devise experiments, investigations to probe them

Helping slow learners

The slow learning child or the one who has learning difficulties will need the teacher to exercise certain skills and strategies in presenting material and in making classroom learning accessible. These will include:

- some individual attention;
- specially selected resource materials;
- careful explanations and instructions;
- clear speech;
- avoiding the child being labelled;
- willingness to praise and encourage;
- ability to break work up into manageable units.

But the teacher will need to do more than this: she will need to provide *a context for learning* within the classroom which provides the right *climate* in which youngsters with learning difficulties can flourish. Attempt Task 61 and then read the passage which follows it.

Task 61 Defining a suitable climate for the slow learner

Give some thought to what we have called a suitable climate or context for learning for the slow learner in the infant school. What are the constituents of such a climate? List what you think they are and then read on. Compare your list with the items mentioned in the quotation below.

The following quotation is an imaginary conversation with an experienced special needs educator, in which he outlines what he believes are the challenges for a suitable climate for classroom achievement.

> 'Slow learners need, above all, security. I believe this is best achieved in small schools, where children remain with one teacher all day – so the traditional infant school is ideal in that sense. Security provides the diffident child with opportunities to develop self-confidence and stand up for him or herself. Children, even at an early age, have to become decision makers. In the kind of class I have outlined change, too, can be taken on board because the teacher can make it happen slowly. Of course, part of the security is dependent upon the teacher defining clearly what is and what is not acceptable behaviour; and in being *consistent* in her own behaviour.
> Slow learners need to make relationships, too. They must learn to work with other children co-operatively; to accept their own

imperfections and learn that others are brittle as well. And every child with special needs, and these children tend to have a poor self-concept, every child must develop an individual identity by taking responsibility – for example, for classroom chores.

It is crucial that in class, teachers relieve the pressure on children. Children with special needs often have a lot to cope with outside school. So they must feel that the school can relieve them of those burdens for a few hours each day. Not that this excuses them from learning to finish tasks or from meeting deadlines. Indeed, the teacher will have to work hard but sensitively to increase concentration spans and 'stickability'.

Finally, I think, the classroom must be a place where these children experience success. If they have handicaps, they must be realistic about them. But they must feel a sense of achievement and of incremental growth. How else can they have anything resembling hope?'

As a footnote to this section perhaps it is worth saying that the approaches advocated here will have spin-offs for one's whole teaching, not just for those aspects of it as they relate to children with special learning needs. If you wish to follow up these subjects you might care to look at Wallace (1983) and Clark (1986).

Unit 16

INTEGRATION IN CURRICULUM BUILDING

'The general progress of children and their competence in the basic skills appear to have benefitted where they were involved in a programme of work that involved art and craft, history and geography, music and physical education and science, as well as language, mathematics and religious education.' HMI (1982)

Such a programme of work is often known as 'Integrated Studies', 'project' work, 'theme' work or 'topic' work. It appears that when working in this way, on 'topics', children gain pleasure from the discovery of new things and use and develop their basic skills in reading, writing and number work. The children themselves may not realise that they are working mathematically or practising writing skills; they may even think they are 'playing' and not consider 'topic' to be 'work' at all – consequently an integrated or topic-based approach usually generates quite a lot of enthusiasm. This view came over most forcefully in taped conversations by children collected by the Schools Council project 'Developing Pupils' Thinking Through Topic Work' (1981–1983). The idea of integration isn't a new one. The philosopher John Dewey built a whole system of education around the project. Sixty years ago 'concentration of studies' became popular: a special topic was chosen as a 'core' and other subjects were built around it. Forty years later, Plowden (1967) still stressed that 'children's learning does not fit into subject categories. The younger the children the more undifferentiated their curriculum will be. Even for older children subjects merge and overlap'. To some extent the rise of middle schools put the clock back by re-emphasizing subjects and encouraging staff to be specialists. But research such as that carried out for the DES Teacher Education Project (Kerry 1982) has suggested that the cognitive demand made upon pupils and the quality of lessons may be measurably better in integrated as opposed to subject-based lessons even in the secondary school. It must remain even more true for infants.

To some extent the case for integrated approaches and the implications for lesson planning (ie the identification of the knowledge, skills and concepts to be learned by pupils) have been discussed in Units 10 and 13 above. Here we shall address ourselves to matters of detail rather than to principles and methods. The fundamental question relates to the initial choice of a suitable topic or topics.

Developing criteria for choosing a topic

Precisely what topic you choose to cover in the infant classroom or school depends upon your response to Task 51 in Unit 13 where you set out your own conceptual map of infant education. You should now turn back to that map and review the kinds of topic implied by it. There is a good chance that some or all of the following broad themes will be there:

- Time and change
- Our place in the town/country/world
- Ourselves and how we live
- Others: how and where they live

Task 62 Identifying possible topics for the infant school

Look over your notes from Task 51 in Unit 13. Compare your conceptual map and the themes implied by it with the four broad topics above. Add to this list anything you consider important.

Once the teacher has decided on the broad curriculum area to be covered, she may choose a specific topic. Her choice may be guided by these considerations:

- *The children.* If a child or a group of children shows a particular interest in a theme, this may be an appropriate start to a topic.
- *Future events/current events.* Sometimes an important event is impending, eg a school trip, concert, or visit by a celebrity to the locality. Perhaps something in the news has fired the imagination: great sporting achievements, advancements in space travel, or alternatively disasters, natural (eruption of a volcano) or man-made (the 'Challenger' disaster).

- *Television*. A particularly good educational television programme can spark off interests leading to a topic or project.
- *The teacher herself*. She may have a particular interest in a theme, and will obviously feel enthusiastic and confident about exploring it with her class, providing information and resources from her existing knowledge and, hopefully, discovering new things with the children too.

Developing the topic to include different curriculum areas

Obviously, the first thing to remember is that each and every area of the curriculum need not be represented in *every* topic undertaken. The credibility of a topic should not be stretched beyond all limits simply to include all the areas. Only the more appropriate areas demand inclusion.

The teacher needs to note, however, which areas are covered in each topic, as a balance needs to be maintained overall. Consequently, if maths (which some teachers find difficult to integrate) does not form part of the topic, the teacher needs to integrate it into the next one if possible or otherwise to provide number activities. The new introduction to Cockcroft (1982) actually stressed that mathematics should be a means of communication 'to represent, to explain and to predict'; which suggests that it really ought to be related to other curriculum areas where possible.

Other areas lend themselves more easily to integration – language (in particular); reading, writing, listening and speaking, also drama; art and craft; environmental study (including scientific, geographical and historical aspects); music and songs on various themes; social, moral and religious education (in sharing and working together on topics as well as in learning activities and gaining information) and PE (through movement in dance in particular).

Perhaps the best way to illustrate how a topic can be built up is to use some lesson notes taken from the Schools Council project already referred to above. The notes give some insight into both the thinking of the teacher and her methods of working.

Topic: Ourselves

No. of children:	33
Age of children:	Six- and seven-year-olds
Duration:	First two/three weeks of term; twice/three times weekly

Relationship to other schemes of work in terms of:

Continuity/Contiguity

Although the theme of 'Ourselves' will serve as an introductory topic, it will run throughout the entire period to the extent that in the basic mathematics topic of 'measuring' improvised units will be provided by the children themselves using hand-spans, feet, etc.

The theme will also recur in some Art and Craft work, as we will be exploring techniques involved in the making of garments, e.g. printing, weaving, embroidery and applique.

The following topic of 'Water' will also continue the theme of 'Ourselves' to some extent, as it will be introduced as something we need in order to live, in addition to food, clothes, etc.

Aims

To enable the children to gain a general knowledge of geographical, historical and social aspects of their local environment, leading to an understanding of the world beyond.

To give the children the opportunity to paint and experiment with various media in Art and Craft.

To enable the children to acquire knowledge about people and their environment, past and present.

To help the children develop the ability to make reasoned judgements concerning choice of relevant information and a critical attitude towards own experience and that of others.

Objectives

To give the children the opportunity to acquire knowledge and information from verbal material (i.e. stories told to them by grandparents).

To add to the children's general knowledge of other times.

To stimulate the children's imaginative and creative techniques (through adventure story).

To give the children the means of expressing their thoughts and viewpoints through painting and collage in art and craft.

Content

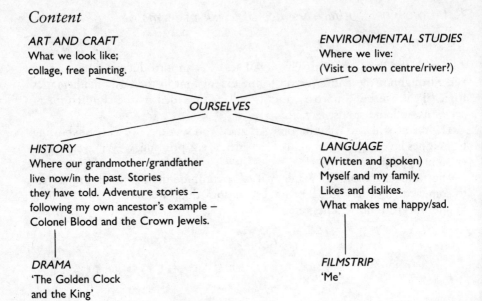

ART AND CRAFT
What we look like;
collage, free painting.

ENVIRONMENTAL STUDIES
Where we live:
(Visit to town centre/river?)

OURSELVES

HISTORY
Where our grandmother/grandfather
live now/in the past. Stories
they have told. Adventure stories –
following my own ancestor's example –
Colonel Blood and the Crown Jewels.

LANGUAGE
(Written and spoken)
Myself and my family.
Likes and dislikes.
What makes me happy/sad.

DRAMA
'The Golden Clock
and the King'

FILMSTRIP
'Me'

Lesson plans: 1 Integrated approach to the theme of 'Ourselves', 'Me', language, (written and spoken), art and craft.

Monday, 6th October:	11.00 am – 12.00 noon
	1.15 pm – 2.35 pm
No. of children:	19
Age of children:	Six- to seven-year-olds

Objectives

- To encourage the children to reflect on their own appearances and circumstances, and how they differ from other people's, and to record their thoughts.
- To give the children the opportunity to consider their own feelings and opinions about things which they do every day and to assess their likes and dislikes from these occurrences.
- To give the children a light-hearted look at personal pronouns through verse and an opportunity for oral involvement by repetition.

- To allow the children to work with a variety of media through painting and collage, thus giving them an opportunity to work in both two and three dimensions.
- To encourage the children to observe critically in order to achieve realistic results in painting by the use of a mirror.

Organisation

The children will work individually, grouped around two tables, after an introductory discussion when the children will be seated on the floor by my chair for closer contact. I hope that the discussion with the children will last about 20 minutes in order that the children's thoughts will be clarified.

Learning Experiences

'Me' – Introduction

This will take the form of a fairly informal discussion with the children (although I will insist from the beginning that they must raise their hands to be asked for answers to questions to avoid children calling out answers, as certain children would dominate the discussions if this was the case). I will ask questions about the children themselves (Where do you live? What are your brothers/sisters called? How old are they? Have you got any pets? What are they called? What do you like doing best in school? . . . at home? . . . in the evenings? . . . at weekends? What is your favourite food? . . . place? . . .What do you like doing best? What is your favourite television programme?)

Development

The children will then be asked to write about themselves: what they are called, what they look like, and other details about their lives that we have talked about in the discussion.

When the children have finished their writing, they can paint a picture of themselves, using powder paints; and they will be encouraged to use their reflection in a mirror as a guide, as a self portrait is a very difficult assignment!

'My Feelings' – Introduction

(Probably pm) This will be a short discussion. Again, it will be fairly informal and I will ask the children about things which make them happy and things which make them feel sad (it could be something they do or see, or perhaps hear).

Development
I will then give the children two pieces of paper, both in the shape of a bag; one will be headed 'MY HAPPINESS BAG' and the other 'MY SADNESS BAG'. They will then write down the things which evoke those emotions within themselves.

'What I look like' – Introduction
I will discuss the uses of the collage material with the children by asking for suggestions (what could I use to make an eye, etc.?)

Development
The children will then make a collage of themselves, i.e. 'Me', using the collage materials provided.

Conclusion (the whole theme) 'Me, Myself and I'

I will read two short verses to the children, one entitled 'Three Guests' and the other 'Me, Myself and I' which will introduce the use of personal pronouns. I will encourage the children to join with me in saying the verses after I have repeated them.

Materials

Paper; pencils; drawing paper; collage materials; adhesive; spatulas; paint brushes; 'happiness' and 'sadness' bags; paint; poems.

2   Ourselves – My Relative and Ancestor: concept and language work

Wednesday, 8th October: 11.00 am – 12.00 noon
No. of children: 19
Age of children: Six- to seven-year-olds

Objectives

- To give the children a sense of their orientation in time by developing an understanding of the words 'relative' and 'ancestor'.
- To link the work to the children's everyday experience through the focus on clothes worn by our ancestors in certain periods and those worn today.

- To stimulate the children's imaginations and evoke their viewpoint on the moral questions I will raise.
- To give the children an opportunity to use the knowledge they have gained to write (a) about the meaning of relatives and ancestors and (b) the story of the attempt to steal the Crown Jewels (in a partly closed learning situation, i.e. by use of workcards).

Organisation

The children will be seated around my chair on the floor in order that I can show them the charts I have made concerning relatives and ancestors and discuss them in a fairly informal way. I will then read to them the story of my ancestor, Colonel Blood, and his attempt to steal the Crown Jewels. Following this, the children will return to their seats which will be grouped around two tables, to complete the written work on the theme.

Learning Experiences

Introduction

I will have a discussion with the children, using prepared charts to illustrate the meaning of relatives and ancestors. We will then discuss the differences in clothes worn by my ancestor in the 17th century and those worn today and the implications for seasonal differences in weather conditions. They will be able to touch some very old garments and compare their materials and textures with their own.

Development

I will then read to the children the story of the theft of the Crown Jewels by my ancestor. This will be followed by questions which will challenge the children's thinking on the moral aspect of stealing. We will then discuss the consequences of Colonel Blood's actions, and decide if we think the correct action was taken by the King.

Conclusion

The children will then be asked to write about what they have heard and discussed with the aid of a workcard:

Our Relatives and Ancestors

Someone who belongs to our family *now* is called our r..........
Someone who belonged to our family a *long, long time ago* is called our
a..........
I have some relatives, one of them is my ....
One of Miss Tollitt's ancestors was called Colonel B.........
He tried to steal the C.......... J.......... from the T.......... of ....
This is the story of what he did.

Materials

Two large charts; one small chart; the story of Colonel Blood and the Crown
Jewels; paper; pencils; pictures of the Crown Jewels; workcards.

3   Ourselves – My Relatives and Ancestors: an approach through art and craft

Wednesday, 8th October:	1.15 am – 2.35 pm
No. of children:	19
Age of children:	Six- to seven-year-olds

Objectives

- To link with the morning's work on the Crown Jewels and prepare some 'props' for the drama lesson tomorrow which involves the children taking part as kings.
- To promote the children's manipulative skills through skilful use of scissors, spatulas etc.
- To give the children the opportunity to work with a variety of media, i.e. paint, coloured tissue paper, metallic paper.

Organisation

The children will begin the session on the floor. I will demonstrate how they
are to cut out their crown shape from the templates. We will then discuss the
possible uses of the materials provided to decorate the crown. They will then
move into their seats grouped around two tables.

Learning Experience

Introduction

This will take the form of instruction by me, concerning the cutting out, assembling and decoration of the crowns. I will ask the children for suggestions concerning the decoration, and then will demonstrate how the coloured tissue can be crumpled into ball shapes which can then be fixed to the crown by adhesive.

Development

The children will then proceed to make a crown each, using the materials provided; and I will help individual children if any problems arise.

Materials

Metallic paper; templates; pencils; tissue paper; adhesive, glue pots; spatulas; scissors; gold and silver crayons; beads.

4   Ourselves – Our Ancestors: The King and the Golden Clock (drama)

Thursday, 9th October:	9.30 am – 10.00 am
No. of children:	33
Age of children:	Six- to eight-year-olds

Objectives

- To link with the 'Ourselves' theme of ancestors concerning kings and stolen possessions.
- To promote the children's expressive movement and interpretation of a story using their bodies.
- To give the children a sense of empathy and personal involvement in a story through taking on the role of a character/characters in that story.

Organisation

The children will begin the session grouped around my chair, seated on the floor, and we will discuss the theme of the drama for about five minutes. They will then spread out a little to begin the dramatic activity.

Learning Experiences

Introduction

During this discussion, I will tell the children briefly what the theme of the story is. (Does it remind you of another story you have heard this week?)

Development

I will then begin the drama session by asking the children to perform certain actions which will appear in the actual story, for example, creeping quietly, cutting away undergrowth in a forest, etc. I will demonstrate these actions where necessary.

Conclusion

After practice in the various actions, I will begin to read the story and the children will respond with the appropriate movement. When taking part as kings they will wear the crowns which they have made. Throughout the story I will provide the appropriate musical accompaniment on percussion instruments.

Materials

Story, crowns, drum, cymbal, wood block.

Some advantages of an integrated view of knowledge at the infant level

Integration at the infant level means that the teacher can start from the child, from his point of view, taking note of his past experiences at home and school to provide activities which will have some relevance for him. In our fast moving world children need a flexible, independent approach to life. They need to think critically, sift through information and solve problems for themselves (Frey 1983). With an integrated view of knowledge, they will be more able to make sense of the world in its ever-changing complexity.

It has been suggested (Sidler 1974) that 'the world as we see it is a mental picture, making sense as a whole . . . It follows that the sort of integration to be aimed at is in the mind of the pupil.' The child needs a world picture that makes sense *as a whole*, and any new experiences need to fit into that picture. The teacher needs to provide experiences which will enable integration to expand the picture 'pushing out bridges from it to adjacent islands'.

Working together and sharing ideas, experiences and equipment are necessary features of the infant school, all of which are developed to a high level through integration of areas of knowledge in project work. In the vertically grouped class, which is a common organisational feature of infant schools today, 'topic' work provides a common theme, a common bond for a large age group to work on together. Here, an integrated view of knowledge means that the children can work on tasks related to a theme at their own level, and this is particularly important in classes with wide age and ability ranges.

Resources for topic work

Finally in this Unit we turn our attention to resources. Success in topic work relies on a good choice of resources, which should include

- first-hand experiences for children;
- access to good books, good libraries and museum resources;
- effective visual aids, including posters, films, slides and television.

Of these, the first two are discussed elsewhere in this book. Below is a list of addresses from which high quality visual material may be obtained.

Tecmedia Ltd, 5 Granby Street, Loughborough LE11 3LD (Educational Software: A Creator's Handbook)

5–12, 2 Church Street, Seaford, Sussex BN25 1HD (Primary software specialists)

Artec Ltd, Salewheel House, Ribchester, Preston, Lancashire PR3 3XU (Save on Science catalogue)

Educational Foundation for Visual Aids, The George Building, Normal College, Bangor, Gwynedd LL57 2BZ

Trans-Ed Copying Services, 15 Ladybower Close, North Hykeham, Lincoln LN6 8EX

M R H Systems & Software, 20 Highfield Road, Kidderminster, Worcester DY10 2TL

London Urban Studies Service, c/o Notting Dale, Urban Studies Centre, 189 Freston Road, London W10 1YH

Council for Environmental Education, School of Education, University of Reading, London Road, Reading RG1 5AQ (environmental resource information)

Franklin Watts, 12A Golden Square, London W1R 4BA

Philip Green Educational Ltd, 112A Alcester Road, Studley, Warwickshire B80 7NR

For teachers, resources ought to include access to:
Child Education journal
Junior Education journal
Schools Council (1981–1983) Topic Work Resource Bank

These items listed all contain material of interest to teachers trying to improve their own skills as well as indicating or containing material for direct classroom use.

Unit 17

REINFORCING LEARNING THROUGH DISPLAY

Overheard in the corridor:

'I've looked into that classroom every day for two years. The display changes every two weeks, but it always ends up looking the same!'

This unkind but apt remark about a colleague exposes just one of the problems facing the teacher who, correctly, wants to use the display as a medium to encourage learning but who fails to get the basic principles and techniques right. There is no 'right' kind of display, and no 'right way' of mounting one – but there are common errors. Repetition of style is just one. Here are some more:

- Poor mounting of pictures or work.
- Inept choice of colours.
- Items hung crookedly.
- Poor labelling.
- Prohibitions on the children which prevent touching and so experiencing the display.

Task 63 Spotting errors in display

From your observation and experience make a list of errors in display technique. Resolve not to commit any of these mistakes! Then think positively through the rest of this Unit of the book.

To exploit classroom resources to the full, by providing displays which reinforce learning, requires a great deal of planning and imagination on the part of the teacher. In this section, we will discuss *how* display can be used as a tool to reinforce learning and in doing so, we will provide some specific ideas and methods. Your job will be to extend your knowledge and practise in this skill by using these simply as starting points.

Providing a stimulating environment

At the start of the school year, confronted with an empty classroom, the teacher is faced with the task of creating a stimulating, inviting environment for her class to enter! Very often, physical considerations seem over-riding and insurmountable: peeling plaster on walls, shortage of actual display space, ancient furniture, very high windows providing a dark dreary atmosphere (especially if the room is north facing and never feels the benefit of a bright sunny afternoon!)

Nevertheless, the resourceful teacher may overcome these handicaps by the use of bright, colourful pictures – springboards for planned topics perhaps, and displays using a common theme, for example, a colour display, an 'old things' table, a 'things with holes in' display and an 'all these reflect' display table. Then, as the weeks progress, the picture stimuli can be replaced by the children's own work.

 ### Task 64 Assessing classroom impact

On the first day of the term (or school year) walk into your own classroom or that of a colleague and try to survey the room *as if you were a child*. What would 'catch your eye', if anything (bearing in mind the difference in child eye-level and adult eye-level)? Write down as many ways as possible in which you could make it more stimulating. Decide on specific areas in the room where improvement is obviously needed eg would you feel comfortable sitting on the carpet in the book corner?

A new item brought into the classroom each day by the teacher, no matter how small, will help sustain the children's interest. They will be stimulated by a constantly changing environment. But the use of display does not end there. The well-planned display can reinforce and extend their learning further. Displays are not to be put up one day and taken down the next, they must be exploited. The following paragraphs offer some ideas and suggestions.

Developing and reinforcing reading, language and thinking skills through display

Reading a story in the infant classroom is a daily event. This is often followed up by paintings by the children of scenes from the story. Quite often a display is mounted showing the story's main event, or the story in sequence (usually in collage form or in figures and objects painted by the children). Pictures such as these are an excellent way of encouraging children to talk. The teacher must exploit this to develop children's skills and her own.

Skill 1 Discussion

The teacher can ask the children 'what was the story about?' (asking them to identify the main event); 'Why does the little boy look upset?' 'What had the shop keeper told him?' 'Why do you think he said that?' 'How do you think it happened?' etc (asking for the children's own interpretations of the story).

Skill 2 Sequencing and prediction

If a story has been displayed in sequence the children can be encouraged to note the progression from one situation to another and the teacher can focus on the importance of sequence through a simple example – do you put on your coat first or your jumper and trousers? The story illustrated in the wall display could be made in miniature on pieces of card for the children to organize in sequence and retell the story using the cards as visual aids. The teacher herself could tell the story, leaving out the last card, and ask the children to predict the ending.

Skill 3 Questioning

Questioning skills could be developed by illustrating the use of 'question words' using the story sequence as a 'reminder': who? what? where? when? how? (The children can be encouraged to ask each other, and find out the vast amount of detail to be discovered by the use of a few short, simple words).

Developing and reinforcing concepts in early number work through display

What follows are some typical examples of very simple classroom strategies for using display to reinforce mathematical learning.

Shapes (two-dimensional)

A display of two-dimensional shapes showing examples from the classroom or home, or pictures of those shapes occurring in the environment, helps to develop the concept of shape. This display can be coupled with a great deal of practical work to familiarise the children with the various shapes. However, reinforcement in the form of a story display would fix the concept of the shapes triangle, square, rectangle, pentagon, hexagon and octagon quite firmly as follows:

The Story of Simon Shape

On Monday, Simon Shape woke up as a triangle, feeling very hungry. All day long, he didn't stop eating. And he went to bed feeling very full indeed.

Monday   triangle   (Head is made from a circle with a circle for eyes. Semi-circles form the hands and feet and arms and legs are made from rectangles).

On Tuesday when he woke up, he had grown another side and had become a square. All the sides were equal in length. But he still felt hungry and ate just as much as he had on Monday.

Tuesday   square

On Wednesday he awoke to find that two of his sides had grown longer than the other two. His body looked very long! But still he carried on eating, and this time he ate even more than he had on Tuesday.

Wednesday   rectangle

On Thursday he discovered that he had grown yet another side. He now had five sides and was a pentagon! But greedy Simon carried on eating and eating!

Thursday   pentagon

By Friday he had grown another side. As a hexagon he had six sides now. But still he continued to eat more and more.

Friday   hexagon

So that, by the time Saturday morning came, he had grown not one more side, but two, and was now an octagon with eight sides! His eating continued until by Saturday night he felt so ill he had to send for the Shape Doctor, who put him on a very strict diet!

Saturday   octagon

The diet was so strict (Simon wasn't allowed any food at all, and could drink only water) that by Sunday night Simon was back to three sides again – a triangle! He felt much better and promised the doctor that he would never be so greedy again.

Sunday   triangle

(This story also reinforces the spellings and order of the days of the week).

Length

What better display than a permanent one in the playground? A life-size outline painting of one of the dinosaurs on the playground surface (in paint used for marking out netball courts, tennis courts etc) would serve to reinforce the concept of length.

Paintings of two or three animals of today would also be a good comparison to make.

Time

A very simple illustration of a nursery rhyme like Hickory Dickory Dock showing a particular time which the children are immediately familiar with, can help with work on the time. It provides an instant answer: 'What time does this clock-with-the-mouse-running-down show?' And the children would have the correct time straight away – and feel that they could tell the time: instant confidence. All the other o'clocks are simply learnt afterwards.

Cardinal number

Many nursery rhymes and songs can be displayed in picture form to reinforce cardinal number eg: Ten Green Bottles, Five Little Speckled Frogs, Five Little Monkeys etc.

Ordinal number

Songs and rhymes can be used in the same way and displayed with *first*, *second* and *third* labels for the various figures or sequences. This can be reinforced through many classroom activities. Thus, after a baking session the recipe could be written out together with appropriate pictures for the different stages:

1st First we weighed all the ingredients
2nd Second we mixed the butter and the sugar etc.

The finished product (the biscuits) could be displayed using 'stuffed shapes' for a three-dimensional effect. These are simply made by cutting paper in the shape of the biscuits. Two paper shapes are placed together, stapled almost all the way round the circumference leaving a gap for the 'biscuit' to be stuffed with newspaper. The gap is then closed and the two sides stapled together.

Size

Size comparison needs practical development and visual reinforcement. An idea for reinforcing size differences once again stems from well-known stories – Goldilocks and the Three Bears, Three Billy Goats Gruff. Once displayed in picture collage form, the differences become obvious. Size vocabulary can then be learnt easily by the children: small/tiny/medium/middle-sized/large/huge.

Money (addition, multiplication and subtraction)

Practical handling of money is an excellent way of reinforcing the concept of the value of money. Everyday situations can be recreated in the classroom situation, whereby the children can experience purchasing goods and receiving change. For example, a class shop or a game as follows:

The Bus Conductor Game

A display is first mounted, of a bus made by the children and a bus route. (*Ordinal number* comes in once again here, also *addition*, and *multiplication*, for example counting in twos, threes or fours, fives etc, depending how much each fare stage goes up in price).

The Bus Route

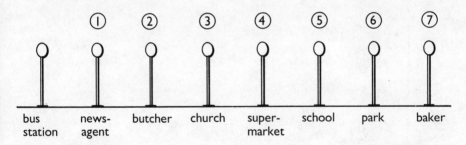

| bus station | news-agent | butcher | church | super-market | school | park | baker |

Each fare stage is 2p.

The bus route

The children can set out their chairs as if they are sitting on a bus and one child wears the bus conductor's bag which is made from card and holds the ready made bus tickets coin-stamped with all the different possible fares, and some change in plastic money. The children have to look at the route display, state their destination, and tender the money. The conductor has to supply the ticket and change if needed. It can be seen here that addition or multiplication will be needed to work out the fare. A journey to the church would cost either $2p + 2p + 2p = 6p$.

or $3 \times 2p = 6p$ (looking at the stage – 3rd, therefore 3×2)
or $2, 4, 6 = 6p$ (counting on in two's).

A subtraction sum would then be needed if change was required.

Pictorial representation

Always an excellent way of reinforcement after a great deal of practical work, eg if eye colour had been studied by a class, physical means could first be employed – a line of the blue-eyed children
– a line of the green-eyed children
– a line of the brown-eyed children
– a line of the hazel-eyed children
– a line of the grey-eyed children

This could be painted; for example coloured cubes could be used to represent the children: seven blue cubes, five green cubes etc in columns in descending order of occurrence.

Then finally, to show complete understanding, coloured squares could be glued to a chart, or cut out eyes in the correct colours could form a pictogram.

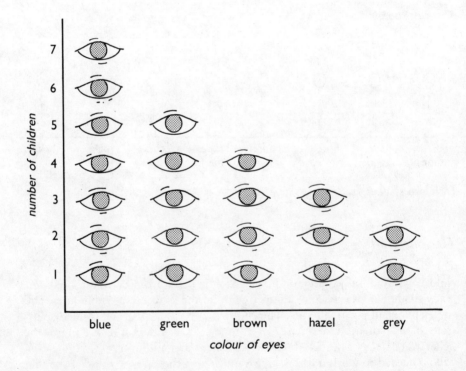

The children could be asked questions concerning the pictograms to test their understanding:

Which colour of eye is most common?
How many children have hazel eyes?

Any further work concerning sets and subsets (eg using Venn circles)

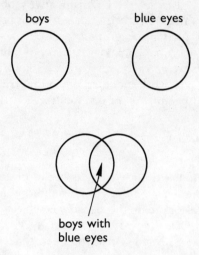

could be presented pictorially following the practical work, to reinforce the concept.

Task 65 Devising number-based displays

Look at the paragraphs above concerning early number work. Choose two sections that relate to your own class and provide an example in each case of how display could reinforce the concepts involved. The choice of a familiar story to illustrate an idea, or a typical real life event (eg a bus ride) could provide possible starting points for the display. Remember that *beginning with situations or objects familiar to the children is a crucial skill of the infants' teacher*: unfamiliarity may block understanding. Plan out the displays you would use and if possible try them out in your own classroom. Don't forget to sound out children's opinions of the displays.

Some points to remember about display using different levels and dimensions

All levels of the classroom can be used. Wall space can be covered with two-dimensional figures and pictures, and three-dimensional ones which make them more eye-catching. Boxes can be stapled to the wall and work mounted on them for a 3D effect. Figures can be made 3D by slight padding with newspaper at the back. Pieces of written work can be mounted in pairs, folded down the centre and mounted to form a triangular structure. In addition to wall space, the floor to ceiling space can be used by imaginative mobiles, or constructions from ground level upwards. (Head clearance needs to be considered with any suspended work, and anything at ground level obviously needs to be away from the entrance to the room or passages between tables.) Hanging screens can be used to fill in between space, or string can be suspended from floor to ceiling in a fan shape and work mounted on to the string. Washing-lines are a popular means of suspending work or mobiles.

Using drapes

Some teachers prefer to use drapes to act as backdrops to displays, and some LEAs seem to insist on them! Nothing is more boring than displays mounted similarly on every occasion: to do this defeats the object of the exercise, which is to attract attention. The key word is *impact*. Nevertheless, drapes can be used effectively if used sparingly. Any type of material can be employed for this purpose. In fact a variety of textures complement each other in many displays. Drapes can be used in three ways; as a backing to a display on wall or table; as a screen on which to pin work (with a piece of dowel in the hem like a curtain); to create an actual visual aid eg a waterfall using silver paper etc.

Straining for quality

There is a definite need to set high standards in displays the teacher uses to reinforce concepts or skills. Display is not window dressing; it is necessary to sustain quality of presentation in order to encourage children to value and appreciate quality. Just as children's work which is well done deserves to be attractively and neatly mounted for display, so teacher-made resources (such as a cut out animal with descriptive words written on it and used as a mobile), teacher made games, or any visual aids also need to be the best which the individual teacher can produce. It is *not* necessary to be an artist in order to produce a quality display – but it does help if you can cultivate these qualities:

- Neatness
- Inventiveness
- Colour sense
- Environmental awareness

Then all your displays will be *nice*!!
Finally in this section try to summarize your thoughts by tackling Task 66.

Task 66 Reflecting on display

You have been put in charge of display work in your school. The head has called a staff meeting. She has asked you to talk for about 15–20 minutes about the value of display in children's learning. Prepare an outline of the talk you will give.

TABLE 39 Some do's and don'ts for display work

DO	DON'T
Use a staple gun, double-sided sellotape, map tacks	Use drawing pins, dress-making pins, sellotape
Use plenty of children's work	Be afraid to make your own quality contributions to display (figures, pictures etc)
Encourage children to bring exhibits	Ban touching and participation
Use clear lettering 　Letraset 　stencils 　marker pens 　bold colours	Mis-spell words Leave out words Omit labels Write too small, too thin Use pale colours
Plan displays to tie in with current curriculum	Put up an irrelevant display 'because it looks nice'
Leave displays in place for a reasonable time. Change a section of your display work at a time, for continuity	Take displays down after two days; or leave them up for a term or more

Unit 18

USING ANCILLARY HELP EFFECTIVELY

Parents

'Teachers hide behind high walls, drawing a line between themselves and those who are not professionally engaged in education – the parents of the children they teach' (Nichol 1982).

Although this may be true in some cases, a recent survey of parental involvement in primary schools (Cyster et al 1980) showed that good practice as advocated by Plowden, Bullock, and more recently, the Thomas Report (TES 18.1.85) is on the increase. The work of Wolfendale in 1983 illustrated this further with many examples of innovation and initiative: school-based 'outreach work' by home visitors or liaison teachers, parents' resource centres, for example Newham Parents' Centre, toy libraries and home-based reading programmes (Smith 1984).

Unfortunately not all types of parental involvement are as enlightened. In some schools, teachers are willing to allow parents to help only with fund-raising to provide equipment and additional facilities. Any opportunities they are offered may consist of anything from mending books and washing paint pots to helping with the construction of a rabbit hutch, or even a swimming pool! This type of involvement does little to augment the educational understanding of parents. A better aim is surely to form a partnership between home and school whereby parents can play an active part in school life, giving support and gaining understanding in a constructive way. A closer relationship with their child's teacher should ensure that all the child's needs are understood and consequently catered for, in social, physical, emotional and educational terms – altogether, a better understanding of the child must lead to better, more appropriate provision. In some cases, a few minutes' chat with a parent concerning a disturbing feature of her child's behaviour over a period of time can often reveal a simple cause which, once known, can be acted upon in a constructive way to help the child concerned. For this reason, the teacher must try to convey the impression of availability at all times to parents. Working in a partnership can only benefit the teacher, the parent and the child.

Task 67 Making yourself available to parents

How do you think you can make yourself 'available' to the parents of the children you teach? Consider the past academic year (if you are still in training, ask one of the teachers in your current school about her practice, and make her the subject of your study).

On how many occasions have the parents of the children in your class been 'invited' into school? (Include here parents' evenings, open days, school parties, school trips etc).

Have parents made the effort to come in and see you personally, concerning their child's progress or any problems he may have had, on occasions other than those 'invited' visits?

In view of your answers to the above, do you feel that you have made the parents of the children in your class welcome or not? If not, attempt to define three strategies for future use which will make you more accessible to them.

The issue of parental involvement has already been discussed briefly in Unit 4 of this book, but because of its importance it might be worthwhile for you to refer back to Task 12 there and then to look at the Table below.

TABLE 40 Some guidelines for a working partnership with parents

The kind of help parents can bring to bear on the partnership depends on their skills, abilities, knowledge and involvement. But the possibilities are limitless:

- A particular day each week can be arranged on which some parents can come in and hear children read, read to children and talk to them.

- A parent with a certain skill, eg in cookery or needlework/other craft work, could take withdrawal groups for practical work which needs a low child/adult ratio. Alternatively, such parents could work together with the teacher to be an 'extra pair of hands' in such activities.

- Where a 'parent's room' is available, some parents prefer to help in skilled but non-professional ways, such as making a catalogue of library books or repairing books, away from the classroom.

- Many practical activities (either together with the teacher in the classroom or taking a withdrawal group) are possible, such as making simple musical instruments and making music.

- Valuable social integration can take place if teachers and parents take children swimming at the local pool or school pool.

- Some parents are experts in their field and can provide very valuable contributions to class projects if they come in and talk to the children about their subject. It brings the subject to life for the children, and is an excellent way of involving parents and opening the doors to the community and its life and work.

- Accompanying a class on a school trip is one valuable means of introducing parents to the idea of involvement with school life. 'I didn't like to ask', 'Could I help?' are often heard amongst parents once they have been approached to come along on a school trip. Being assigned to a group of children for a day means that they quickly become acquainted with at least some of the class, and won't be afraid to come into school to work with the children once they know they are welcome.

- Parents with special interests could arrange to talk to a small group of interested children out of school hours with a view to starting a club with a member of the teaching staff, for example stamp-collecting, or a recorder group.

A quarter of schools responding to a survey by Cyster et al, reported in Smith (1984), were not willing to have parents in their classrooms. Here is a selection of the reasons; how do you react to them?

- Breakdown of confidentiality brought about by parental gossip.
- Behaviour problems resulting from parental presence.
- Criticism of teachers by parents.
- Failure by parents to understand school aims.

Welfare assistants

Welfare assistants are employed by LEAs to look after pupils, for example during lunch breaks. Liaison between teachers and welfare assistants is important, and the two groups may need to discuss any problems particular children may have. Each should know the appropriate actions to take when in sole charge. For example, during the lunch break when the welfare assistants take responsibility, any 'new' children who may be a little unsure of themselves and their new environment may need special attention. Individual pupils may have food allergies which need pointing out; one of them could have been ill during the morning session and may need to be watched carefully for any signs of recurrence; two children may have had a disagreement and may require separating for a period of time until their differences are properly reconciled.

After lunch, the welfare assistant may need to speak with the teacher if anything unusual has occurred, eg an accident, or she may discuss the reactions of any new children over the lunch period. Perhaps one child does not seem to play with any others in the playground – this could be worth mentioning. It is not an opportunity for any disruptive behaviour to be reported back. The use of the teacher as a threat ('I'll tell Mrs . . . at half past one') is not to be encouraged unless the incident is very serious, in which case it requires discussion and possible strategies need to be worked out together for future occurrences. The head, teachers and welfare assistants need to have a common and agreed mode of operation.

Ancillary helpers

In some authorities ancillary helpers are supplied to schools, as part- or full-time employees. They are not trained teachers or nursery officers and are often 'shared' between infant classes on a 'one day each' basis. They are valuable members of the staff in that they can relieve the teacher of routine duties such as mixing paint, mounting art work and making books; and this gives the teacher more time for actual teaching. But more importantly, they can work *together* on topics or in arranging art and craft activities and setting up practical learning situations. The ancillary helper and the teacher *together* can focus on individual needs in a combined effort to encourage and stimulate language development particularly. The ancillary helper will have more time available than the teacher to talk with those children who need extra conversation with an adult. Too much talking with other children can inhibit language development, so this is a very important aspect of the ancillary helper's work. She and the teacher can decide on the children in need of extra help in the development of language skills, based on criteria set up by the teacher. The ancillary helper can then spend certain amounts of time in the classroom with specified withdrawal groups for concentrated attention for talking, reading stories and discussing with them and hearing them read. Obviously, the teacher as the trained professional needs to direct the ancillary's work effectively, but must always listen to the feedback provided by the helper.

NNEB nursery assistants and NNEB students

From time to time a representative of one or both of these groups will form a part of the team which organises classroom life for the children in your charge. NNEB/nursery assistants are often assigned to schools on a regular full-time basis but in a variety of roles. Occasionally, a class teacher may be assisted by a nursery assistant on a permanent basis if she has a child with special needs in her class, for example a partially-hearing child. The nursery assistant will have the task of ensuring that the child concerned is given full attention at all times, except in his free play, explaining what is expected of him in each learning task. More frequently the nursery assistant is shared between classes on a 'one day each' or 'one morning/afternoon each' basis, to assist with routine classroom duties or take small groups. Under no circumstances should she be made to feel that she is simply there for the 'menial jobs'. This should not happen since her expertise far exceeds this.

NNEB students usually visit schools for two or three days a week during training. They are obviously still learning but are nevertheless potential professionals. They will be supervised by tutors in education and in health care. The teacher, along with the college tutors, will liaise about the student's role; and while the teacher gains valuable assistance she will also have to contribute to the student's training and development. NNEB students and trained nursery officers will work confidently alongside the teacher in classroom routines, much as the ancillary helper would. But in addition the NNEB, because of her training in language and number skills and in the social and moral attitudes to be fostered in the children, will be capable of talking with individuals or groups of children who require special attention. She will also work with the teacher on any project work being undertaken in the classroom and will often have a fund of excellent art and craft ideas. Student nursery nurses still in training will, through their contact with tutors who regularly see a variety of ideas in the many schools they visit, have their ideas constantly replenished. An NNEB student or nursery assistant will often take charge of the whole class, and read stories and sing popular infant songs and rhymes with the children from her anthology. This gives the teacher the opportunity to work with individuals who need one-to-one concentrated attention at that time.

The NNEB will also have excellent organisational and managerial skills which, combined with practical knowledge of, for example, cookery will mean that the teacher and nursery assistant can plan cookery sessions. She may supervise groups of children in turn to do all the weighing and mixing. This type of activity is very difficult for the teacher alone to manage successfully. Other practical skills she may have acquired in training can also be combined with the teacher's expertise in, for example, needlework: where two pairs of hands can be desperately needed by a class full of five-year-olds all with needles to thread!

Students from colleges of education or university departments

Any student working in your classroom becomes a member of your classroom team. Students on initial courses of teacher training will share your role as teacher and, at later stages in their training, may even take over the bulk of teaching time for a while. As a class teacher you will need to ensure that the children's education does not suffer; but as a fellow professional you will assist the college or university tutor as part of the student's training team. In this respect you may find some help in Kerry (1982).

A student can often be a stimulating member of the team, someone who can encourage the development of new, fresh ideas in many areas of school life. She may also have an interest which she can share with the children – playing the guitar for example.

The length of time spent in schools by students obviously varies; some colleges send students on school studies one day a week. There will be longer practices, usually for a term, to observe and practise the general work of the teacher, supervising small groups of children, usually to develop project work, and helping the teacher in her integrated day. Sometimes the teacher and student work together very closely and constructively on a project: the IT/INSET (initial training and in-service teaching) experiment at Leicester University was a good example of this (Ashton et al. 1983). A 'problem' was identified and outlined by the teacher which could be concerned with any aspect of the school curriculum. Together the student, teacher and college tutor worked through possible developments of the suggested theme or 'problem' with the children and evaluated their success at the end of the set period of school practice.

If a student is specialising in a particular subject such as environmental studies, there can be excellent opportunities for the student to gain practical experience; for the teacher, who is not a specialist in that area, to learn at her own level; and for the children to extend their normal curriculum diet or range of experience.

Having a student present on teaching practice means that the teacher can withdraw individuals for special help while the student still gains excellent experience of class teaching. At all times there must be the closest co-operation between teacher and student to ensure unity of purpose and procedure.

There can be little doubt that having other adults in the classroom (be they parents, visitors, ancillaries, nursery assistants or students) is broadening for children and helpful to the teacher. With this thought in mind you might like to tackle the last task in this Unit.

Task 68 Using ancillary help effectively

1   Review the help available to you from all the sources mentioned in this Unit. It may help to chart its timing on a year planner, since students tend to come for limited periods or on specific days of the week.

2   Now draw up guidelines to yourself on how you will use each kind of help available.

3   Finally, reflect on the ways in which your teaching may become more of a team effort with you as the team leader. What precisely does this mean for your role?

Unit 19

END-NOTE TO THE TEACHER

In the Units which have preceded this one you have undertaken two major activities. First, through the text and Tables you have shared in the professional wisdom of the many educators who have contributed to the books and journals referred to, or who have participated in the projects mentioned. Second, you have actively participated in the extension of your own professional development by undertaking the range of tasks included in the text. In a very real sense you have been able to decide upon and control the direction of your own in-service training. The time has now come to reflect upon what you have gained.

 ## Task 69 Reviewing your teaching skills

At leisure, look back over the Tasks you have completed. Have any of these Tasks

- caused you to rethink your attitudes and approaches?
- helped to confirm what you regard as sound practice?
- altered your classroom behaviour?
- changed your management or administrative procedures?
- provoked you to discuss your approach or practice with colleagues?
- helped to guide others in your charge?

In short, try to sum up *how* the Tasks have helped you and also to indicate any ways in which they might have been modified. If you would like to send a summary of your deliberations to the authors, to help in the overall evaluation of this book, you would be welcome to do so. Send your comments to

Dr Trevor Kerry (re: Teaching Infants)
Doncaster Metropolitan Institute of Higher Education
Park Road
Mexborough
S Yorkshire   S64 9PJ

Finally, you might like to take a more philosophical view of infant education. Task 70 may help this process by means of a simulation exercise.

Task 70 Reflecting on your philosophy of infant education

Imagine you are applying for a promoted post. The application form requires you to set out in about 500 words your philosophy of infant education. Draft out your response after due reflection.

Unit 20

REFERENCES & FURTHER READING

In part 1 of this Unit you will find the references relating to the main text. Some items among these references are marked with an asterisk. The asterisked items, along with the further reading recommended in the second part of the Unit, will make an excellent reading list for a further professional study of education in the early years of schooling.

1 References

Argyle M 1967 *The psychology of interpersonal behaviour*
Harmondsworth: Penguin

Ashton P, Henderson J, Merritt J, Mortimer D 1983 *Teacher education in the classroom: initial and in-service*
Beckenham: Croom Helm

* Ball F 1977 *The development of reading skills*
Oxford: Basil Blackwell

* Beard R 1967 *An outline of Piaget's developmental psychology*
London: Routledge & Kegan Paul

Bell P, Kerry T 1982 *Teaching slow learners in mixed ability classes*
Basingstoke: Macmillan

* Bennett N 1976 *Teaching styles and pupil progress*
London: Open Books

*   Bennett N, O'Hare E, Lee J 1982
    Mixed age classes in primary schools: a survey of practice
    Lancaster: Centre for Educational Research & Development

*   Bradley H, Eggleston J, Kerry T, Cooper D 1985
    Developing pupils' thinking through topic work: a starter course
    York: Longmans

*   Cast P, 1978 *All the years round*
    Nottinghamshire: Local Education Authority

*   Centre for the Teaching of Reading 1984 *Parental involvement in reading*
    Reading: School of Education Press

    Choat E 1979 'Make maths materialize' Child Education August 1979 p 6

*   Clarke M 1986 *Special educational needs and children under five*
    Birmingham: Educational Review Publications

    Clay M 1972 *The patterning of complex behaviour*
    London: Heinemann

    Cockcroft W H 1982 *Maths counts*
    London HMSO

    Cyster et al (see Smith T 1984)

    Dankworth A 1984 in Fontana D (ed) *The education of the young child*
    Oxford: Basil Blackwell

    Dewhurst W 1985 'Early activities'
    Child Education October 1985 p27, 28, 29

    Downey M, Kelly A 1978 *Moral education*
    London: Harper & Row

    Evans E 1979 'Caring about sharing'
    Child Education December 1979 p 12

*   Fontana D (ed) 1984 *The education of the young child: a handbook for nursery and infant teachers*
    Oxford: Basil Blackwell

    Frey J 1983 'Purposeful projects'
    Child Education September 1983 pp 10, 11

    Froebel F 1967 'The Education of Man' *in* W Van der Eyken *The Pre-School Years* Harmondsworth: Penguin

    Gesell A 1954 *The first five years of life*
    London: Methuen

Gesell A, Ilg F 1946 *The child from five to ten*
London: Hamish Hamilton

* Goldman R 1964 *Religious thinking from childhood to adolescence*
London: Routledge & Kegan Paul

Goldman R 1965 *Readiness for religion*
London: Routledge & Kegan Paul

Goodman Y H 1970 'Using children's miscues for new teaching strategies'
Reading Teacher 23.5 p 455

Gregory R 1980 'More than a story'
Child Education July 1980

* Harlen W 1985 *Primary science – taking the plunge*
London: Heinemann

Harlen W, Osborne R 1985 'A model for learning and teaching applied
to primary science'
J Curr Studs 17.2 pp 133–146

Herdson N 1981 'Don't say it, sing it'
Child Education May 1981 p 27

HMI 1978 *Primary education in England*
London: HMSO

HMI 1982 *Primary survey*
London: HMSO

Horner P 1984 in Fontana D (ed) *The education of the young child*
Oxford: Basil Blackwell

ILEA 1976 *Language for learning* Unit 1
London: Heinemann

ILEA 1985 E.O/S.B.2

Kennedy A 1984 *The psychology of reading*
London: Methuen

Kerry T 1982 'Teachers' identification of exceptional pupils and their
strategies for dealing with them'
Nottingham University: unpublished PhD thesis

* Kerry T (ed) 1983 *Finding and helping the able child*
Bexley: Croom Helm

Kerry T 1984 *Teaching religious education*
Basingstoke: Macmillan

Kerry T 1986 *Invitation to teaching*
Oxford: Basil Blackwell

Lane S 1984 in Fontana D (ed) *The education of the young child*
Oxford: Basil Blackwell

* McPhail P 1982 *Social and moral education*
Oxford: Basil Blackwell

* May N 1984 *in* F Schostak & T Logan *Pupil experience*
Bexley: Croom Helm

Meek M 1982 *Learning to read*
London: Bodley Head

Michael B 1984 'Foundations of writing'
Child Education January 1984 page 10

Milligan S 1968 *Silly verse for kids*
London: Puffin Books

MIMEO undated *Aims and objectives of primary education*
A study by nine headteachers

Montague J 1979 'Not just play'
Child Education October 1979 p 27

Moon C 1985 'Alternative approach'
Child Education October 1985 pp 23, 24, 25

* Moyle D 1984 *The teaching of reading*
London: Ward Lock

Moyles J 1986 'The whole picture'
Child Education March 1986 p 10, 11

Nichol J 1982 'Teachers hide behind high walls'
Child Education October 1982 p 27

Nuffield Science 1967 London: Collins

* Osborn A, Butler N, Morris A 1984 *The social life of Britain's five-year-olds*
London: Routledge & Kegan Paul

Plowden Lady B 1967 *Children and their primary schools*
London: HMSO

Potworowska A, Standfield J 1985 *Kites*: cut-out apparatus book
London: Evans

Reed J, Donaldson M 1979 *Letter links*
Edinburgh: Holmes McDougall

* Rosen H, Rosen C 1973 *The language of primary school children* Harmondsworth: Penguin

Sadler J 1974 *Concepts in primary education* London: George Allen & Unwin

Schola 1982 *Hand in your writing* Scottish Committee of Language Arts in the Primary School

School Curriculum Development Committee 1985 *Topic work resource book* London: SCDC

Smith F 1971 *Understanding reading* London: Holt Reinhart & Winston

Smith T 1984 in Fontana D (ed) *The education of the young child* Oxford: Basil Blackwell

Stenhouse L 1970 *Humanities Curriculum Project Handbook* London: Schools' Council

* Tough J 1977 *Talking and learning* London: Ward Lock

* Van der Eyken W 1967 *The pre-school years* Harmondsworth: Penguin

* Wallace B 1983 *Teaching the very able child* London: Ward Lock

Warnock M 1978 *Special educational needs* (Report of the Warnock Committee) London: HMSO

Wishart T 1980 *Sounds fun* Schools Council & Drake Educational Associates March 1980

Woolfson R 1985 'Show the way' Child Education December 1985

Yardley A 1979 Child Education January 1979 p 15

2 Further Reading

Atkin J, Webb J 1985 *Studyguide 8: Nursery education* Nottingham: School of Education

Bruner J 1980 *Under five in Britain* London: Grant McIntyre

Chazan M, Williams P 1978 *Deprivation and the infant school*
Oxford: Basil Blackwell

Clift P, Cleave S, Griffin M 1980 *The aims, role and deployment of staff in the nursery*
Windsor: NFER

Galton M, Simon B, Croll P 1980 *Progress and performance in the primary classroom*
London: Routledge & Kegan Paul

Garland R 1982 *Computers and children in the primary school*
Sussex: Falmer Press

Jowett S, Sylva K 1986 'Does kind of pre-school matter?'
Educ Res vol 28.1 21-31

Richards C 1982 *New directions in primary education*
Sussex: Falmer Press

Richards C, Holford D 1981 *The teaching of primary science: policy and practice*
Sussex: Falmer Press

Tizard B, Mortimore J, Burchell J 1981 *Involving parents in nursery and infant schools*
London: Grant McIntyre

Whitaker P 1983 *The primary head*
London: Heinemann

Whitbread N 1972 *The evolution of the nursery-infant school: a history of infant and nursery education*
London: Routledge & Kegan Paul